"Ready to Lead?" is a much needed work that adds depth, perspective and practical steps to an ongoing conversation about what diversity in the body of Christ can look like among those of different ethnicities who have reconciled hearts. This book is a must read for anyone who wants to see the Kingdom in its multicolored expression. Dr. Brian Taylor and Dr. Chris Johnson are two voices that have been anointed to speak to the church on this subject with clarity, compassion and conviction.

-Tim Johnson
Senior Pastor Orlando World Outreach Center
Superbowl Champion

Black spiritual leaders are rarely considered by White Christians as their potential pastors.

The agonizing historical bridge to cross is too long, the cultural gap is too wide, and the difference in both group's perspective on America is more distinguishable than "blue" states are from "red". Still, there is not a problem for which the Gospel does not have an answer.

Pastors Brian Taylor and Chris Johnson have mined out and deployed the biblical truths that dismantle the barriers intended to divide; giving conciliatory hope to generational adversaries.

-Brett Fuller
Bishop- Grace Covenant Church, Washington Metropolitan Area
gracecov.org
Chaplain, Washington Commanders

Ready to Lead is a hard-hitting, honest read, that is full of grace and practical advice. It calls us to lean into the messy work of authentic racial reconciliation and not shrink back from the pain of injustice. A must-read for anyone interested in modeling revival - here and now.

-Carl Stauffer, PhD.
Senior Expert, Reconciliation
United States Institute of Peace

"If you can handle an, at times, painfully honest book about the realities of Black leadership in multi-ethnic churches then you'll find *Ready to Lead* to be a wealth of insights and practical wisdom. From a biblical foundation, Brian Taylor and Chris Johnson examine the tough issues Black leaders confront and they detail a redemptive path forward"

-Justin Giboney
Attorney and Political Strategist
President and Co-Founder of And Campaign

Several years ago, Brian, Chris, and I were classmates at Asbury Theological Seminary's Doctor of Ministry program. Since then, they have both become close friends and conversation partners in ministry, church leadership, and theology.

Brian and Chris are passionate about building churches that reflect the diversity of God's Kingdom-something that is evident immediately when you walk into both of their churches. In their new book, *Ready to Lead: Essential Questions for Empowering Black Leadership in the Multiethnic Church*, you will hear their heart for diversity and learn the steps necessary to make this dream a reality in your own church.

I encourage every pastor to read this book as we consider how to build churches that welcome all people and reflect the diversity of the Kingdom. Building a multiethnic church is not easy, but Brian and Chris share well-researched arguments and hard-earned wisdom to help us do it well.

-Steve Murrell, D Min
President and Co-Founder Every Nation

"Leaders like Brian Taylor change the game. He steps up with poise, power and a prayer filled heart. People follow his lead because of the passion and purpose exuding from his life. There is so much good fruit all around him. The Church needs leaders and thinkers like him and Chavonne, and more churches like Every Nation."

-Chris Beard
Lead Pastor, People's Church Cincinnati

Ready to Lead

Essential Questions for Empowering Black Leadership in the Multiethnic Church

BRIAN TAYLOR and CHRIS JOHNSON

WESTBOW
PRESS®
A DIVISION OF THOMAS NELSON
& ZONDERVAN

Copyright © 2023 Brian Taylor and Chris Johnson.

All rights reserved. No part of this book may be used or reproduced by any means, graphic, electronic, or mechanical, including photocopying, recording, taping or by any information storage retrieval system without the written permission of the author except in the case of brief quotations embodied in critical articles and reviews.

WestBow Press books may be ordered through booksellers or by contacting:

WestBow Press
A Division of Thomas Nelson & Zondervan
1663 Liberty Drive
Bloomington, IN 47403
www.westbowpress.com
844-714-3454

Because of the dynamic nature of the Internet, any web addresses or links contained in this book may have changed since publication and may no longer be valid. The views expressed in this work are solely those of the author and do not necessarily reflect the views of the publisher, and the publisher hereby disclaims any responsibility for them.

Any people depicted in stock imagery provided by Getty Images are models, and such images are being used for illustrative purposes only.
Certain stock imagery © Getty Images.

Unless otherwise noted, scripture quotations taken from the (NASB®) New American Standard Bible®, Copyright © 1960, 1971, 1977, 1995, 2020 by The Lockman Foundation. Used by permission. All rights reserved. www.lockman.org

Scripture quotations marked CSB are taken from the Holman Christian Standard Bible®, Used by Permission HCSB ©1999,2000,2002,2003,2009 Holman Bible Publishers. Holman Christian Standard Bible®, Holman CSB®, and HCSB® are federally registered trademarks of Holman Bible Publishers.

Scripture marked (NKJV) taken from the New King James Version®. Copyright © 1982 by Thomas Nelson. Used by permission. All rights reserved.

ISBN: 978-1-6642-8610-8 (sc)
ISBN: 978-1-6642-8612-2 (hc)
ISBN: 978-1-6642-8611-5 (e)

Library of Congress Control Number: 2022922490

Print information available on the last page.

WestBow Press rev. date: 12/27/2022

Contents

Acknowledgments ix
Introduction xi

1   The Wall in the Head 1
2   Nothing New Under the Sun 4
3   The Question of Credibility: Am I Enough to Lead You? 14
4   The Question of Culture: Do I Have to Abandon My Blackness? .. 22
5   The Question of Conscience: Can I Honestly Talk about Issues? ... 35
6   The Question of Currency: Are There Strings Attached? 55
7   The Question of Courage: Are We Ready to Talk? 63
8   The Question of Conviction: Is It Worth the Headache? 70
9   Question of Collaboration: Can We Mutually Submit? 79
10 Modern-Day Examples 91
11 A Fresh Commitment and Warning 98
12 I Still Have Hope 101

Afterword 103
Notes 105

Acknowledgments

If wealth was defined by relationships, then I should be considered one of the wealthiest people alive. So many relationships have played a role in shaping me, my family, and in turn, shaping this book. God has blessed me with a Proverbs 31 wife, Chavonne, and three children who constantly encourage me to be all God has called me to be. Chavonne has pushed me to complete this book and was willing to move from sunny Orlando and start a church with me in a brand-new city. I am grateful for my parents, Frazier and Geneva, who were my first example of what Christians look like. Thank you to my siblings for always believing in me, and even though my big brother is no longer with us, I know nobody cheered me on like he did.

I am grateful for my Every Nation global family, who not only has taught me so much about following Jesus, but have also taught me about being a part of a multiethnic, multicultural, family called the Body of Christ. On the local front, I am grateful for the staff and congregation at Every Nation Cincinnati Church. I am so honored to serve as your pastor and I hope I represented our community well through this book. I also want to thank all the pastors and leaders in Cincinnati who have welcomed my family and our church with open arms. I specifically want to thank our Cincinnati Mosaix family and City Servants.

Lastly, I want to thank every pastor that has poured into me and mentored me over the years: Pastors Tim and LeChelle Johnson, Pastor Steve Murrell, Bishop Brett Fuller, Dr. Rice Broocks, Bishop Steve Coleman, and Bishop Herman Crockett. Thank you to so many more than I have room to acknowledge right now. Just know that your contribution in my life was not in vain.

Brian

First of all I am thankful for God and His amazing grace. I am on a journey in life and ministry that I would've never imagined. I don't deserve to be where I am, and I know God isn't done yet. I want to thank my wife who is a manifestation of God's grace in my life. She has supported, encouraged, and challenged me to be who God has called me to be as a man, husband, father, and pastor.

To my parents, you all ensured I had experiences earlier in life that would expand my perspective of life and reconciliation. Lastly, Divine Unity Community Church, thank you all for being a multiethnic, multicultural, and multigenerational church. Our story has already been miraculous, and I believe God has so much more. Divine Unity isn't just our name, it is our reality and mission.

Chris

Introduction

The Narrative

"Black people will follow a White pastor, but White people will never follow a Black pastor." These piercing words were the response I heard after I shared my dream to lead a multiethnic church. I was in my twenties and working as a campus missionary with Every Nation Churches and Ministries, a global family of churches that values cultural and ethnic diversity. At the time, I was not sure if I would ever lead my own church. But I knew that if I did, I wanted my church to look like what I'd experienced as a young man at Bethel World Outreach Church in Brentwood, Tennessee. A place where you could not tell if it was a Black church or a White church. I wanted it to be a place where people from Asian descent and Latinos could be at home, where people from every nation, tribe, and tongue could worship together in unity. In my eyes, this would be a taste of heaven on earth. So it made sense that when I talked about my future with an older pastor and family friend, this vision of a multiethnic church was what spilled out. His words, however, brought me face-to-face with a sobering reality.

Let me first say that I do believe that White people, or people from any ethnic background, will follow a Black pastor. Chris and I both lead multiethnic churches as Black pastors in our respective cities of Cincinnati, Ohio, and Harrisonburg, Virginia. While it may seem rare at times, we are not unicorns. I (Brian) have deep friendships with several pastors who look like me who are leading very ethnically diverse churches. Every Sunday I walk into the worship service at the church where I pastor in Cincinnati, and I see cultural and ethnic diversity.

I appreciate this pastor bringing up the conversation all those years ago. While I disagree with this well-meaning pastor's opinion that White people will never follow a Black pastor, I have to admit that his words came from a narrative that is all too common. He simply articulated what many pastors and congregants alike have felt. He brought to light what has been discussed behind closed doors, and he concluded what any casual observer of church life in America, and many other places around the world, would easily surmise: *it is possible to embrace the idea of a multiethnic church while rejecting the reality of multiethnic leadership.* This book is about empowering leaders from all ethnic and cultural backgrounds to lead. But in order to do this there are some difficult questions that need to be addressed.

A while back I had an opportunity to share some of my findings from my research about the challenges Black leaders face when leading multiethnic churches with a group of PhD students. I remember a student who pastored in Sri Lanka came to me after and told me something that was eye-opening. Some of the same dynamics that limit Black leadership in many diverse churches in the US are also at play in his homeland. The issues there pertain more to tribalism rather than Black-White challenges, but the basic dynamics are the same. How do we empower leadership in the church from all people groups and not just from groups that have historically been seen as dominant? The message in these pages is for all those who desire to not only see diversity in the pews but also in the pulpits.

Over the last few decades, a multiethnic movement has gained traction in the United States and other parts of the world. In many ways, there is room for optimism because the church in America is waking up to the need for diversity in her congregations. The last twenty years have shown a pattern of growth in the number of multiethnic churches. (We use the term "multiethnic" to describe congregations that have no more than 80 percent of one ethnicity represented. This percentage is widely accepted as the tipping point when other groups outside of the dominant one in a congregation shape the culture and practices of a local church.) In 1998, only 6 percent of all congregations were multiethnic.[1] In a more recent study in 2019, Michael Emerson released new numbers that revealed

---

[1] Emerson.

that 16 percent "of all congregations across all faith groups could be so described."² This is a 10 percent increase.

The statistics discovered by Emerson and his team not only focus on the congregational numbers. They also examined the trends for the pastors leading those congregations. Asian pastors led 3 percent of these multiethnic churches in 1998, and that number has remained relatively the same at 4 percent in 2019. Hispanic-led multiethnic churches went from 3 percent in 1998 to 7 percent in 2019. The biggest jump was with Black pastors, which went from 4 percent in 1998 to 18 percent in 2019. The only decrease recorded in their research was with White pastors, who led 87 percent of multiethnic congregations in 1998 and only 70 percent in 2019.³

While we are seeing more ethnic diversity in many churches in the United States, these numbers alone do not tell the whole story. Michael Emerson commented on his research with less than flattering honesty: "All the growth has been people of color moving into white churches. We have seen zero change in the percentage of whites moving into churches of color.… For the leaders of color who were trying to create the multiracial church movement, they're basically saying, "it doesn't work."⁴ We still have a lot to learn about the barriers and challenges that are unique to Black pastors. My hope is that this book brings this conversation to the table for Black pastors and any leader or congregant who desires to see Black pastors and pastors of all ethnicities empowered to lead in multiethnic congregations. There are Black leaders and leaders of all ethnicities that are ready to bring immense value to congregants of all cultural backgrounds. We, as the body of Christ, will miss out if diverse churches are not led by them.

Just like Brian, I (Chris) also heard similar rhetoric that Black people will follow a White pastor, but White people will not follow a Black pastor. Having a desire to lead a multiethnic church wasn't the most popular thought in the church background I grew up in. However, throughout my spiritual journey, I was afforded opportunities to be in diverse ministry settings. That exposure expanded my theological lens and deepened my gospel conviction to see a picture of heaven in the church,

---

2   Emerson 2020.
3   Excerpted from the Mosaix Global Network newsletter, December 2019.
4   Gjelten, NPR, "Multiracial Congregations May Not Bridge Racial Divide."

with congregations that represented people from different backgrounds and ethnicities.

This book was inspired by countless conversations between me (Chris) and Brian about processing being Black and leading a multiethnic church. We are both devout members of Every Nation, and during our time completing our Doctor of Ministry degrees, our friendship and co-laboring gained significant momentum. We recognize that much of our leadership and perspective came through our personal development as Christians, pastors, and Black men. We have swung on the pendulum of different points of multiethnic ministry in this modern world. There have been times we have felt our Blackness inwardly marginalized. Other times it felt oppressed. There have also been moments of empowerment where our blackness was celebrated and we were given the opportunity to be bridge builders of the unfortunate divide of the white and black church in our American context.

The multiethnic church is not a matter of convenience, but one of conviction. We believe the church is called to be the meeting place where the beautiful unity of Christ is seen as people from different backgrounds, cultures, languages, and experience are one. We are convinced that the multiethnic church must be a work and witness of the Holy Spirit.

The years 2020 and 2021 revealed some deep, dark issues in our country and the church. It revealed that the church at times has perpetuated a society that prefers segregation over reconciliation. To desegregate the church seems like a task too large for anyone to tackle. Desegregation is not the totality of our goal in this book. Our goal is to contribute to the existing conversation about ethnic and cultural diversity in the church and in the church leadership, while inviting others to take this courageous journey. We will aim to recall the scriptures that point towards a unified body of believers striving to reflect the reconciliation of the gospel, as well as the historic and cultural components that make the multi-ethnic church difficult. We are answering the call to lead with a prophetic picture of a reconciled people for the glory of God. It is a courageous journey of spiritual leadership that is not for the faint of heart. It is a journey that will confront principalities, promote healing, and produce fruit for the glory of God, and the witness of Jesus Christ. We are ready to lead. Are you?

Part 1
Historical Perspective

1

The Wall in the Head

> History is not in the past, it is in the present. We take it with us.
> —James Baldwin, *I Am Not Your Negro*

Following World War II, the nation of Germany was divided into different territories. Eastern Germany was a communist state primarily occupied by Soviet forces. Western Germany became a capitalist society and was occupied by the United States, Great Britain, and eventually France. While these territories were geographically close, they couldn't have been further apart ideologically. This division was highlighted by the construction of a wall in Berlin that stood from 1961 to 1989. More than 170 people died trying to cross that wall.

Although I was a little kid during that time, I remember the words of then US President Reagan to the leader of the Soviet Union: "Mr. Gorbachev, tear down this wall." Within two years, the wall came down, and people were able to move freely between Eastern and Western Germany.

Looking back on this historic time, I found it interesting that although the physical wall came down and people had permission to move freely across the borders by 1989, many people continued to live as if the wall still separated them. Some have called this *Maur im Kopf,* or the wall in the head. Even when physical barriers are removed, we erect mental barriers, which lead to separation.

Jesus dealt with the wall that separates us from one another. Few, if any, divides have been as deep as the one that separates Jew from Gentile, yet this wall was dealt with on the cross. Ephesians 2:14–15 says:

> For He Himself is our peace, who made both groups into one and broke down the barrier of the dividing wall, by abolishing in His flesh the enmity, which is the Law of commandments contained in ordinances, so that in Himself He might make the two into one new man, thus establishing peace.

Unfortunately, as good as the news in Ephesians 2 is, churches nevertheless separate according to the way we look or the salaries that we make. Sometimes I wonder if the church still deals with the wall in the head. Some of us are chipping away at the wall; others may not even recognize that a wall exists. Sadly, the church in America has, at times, helped to reconstruct the walls of racial and ethnic separation, both in church buildings and in American culture. James Baldwin once said, "History is not in the past, it is in the present. We take it with us."[5] The church in America has a history. We, as the church, are not limited by the shortcomings of our past, but we must not be blind to them either. There are great books that detail the racial history of the United States and how the church is interwoven in that history. We must come to terms with the fact that these racialized walls faced today have a history, and while things in our society have improved, some of those walls in the head have been brought with us into the present.

On the other hand, we have also seen the power that happens when the people of God live out Ephesians 2 in its fullness. Review the movements from Ephesians 2:14-15 once again: The wall of hostility is torn down, and Christ creates a new humanity. A new people with a divine purpose emerges. That was the product of the gospel according to Ephesians 2: a new ethnicity that does not dismiss our origin, but emphasizes our redemption. The fruit of our redemptive nature in Christ is marked by our relational equity with one another. In the creation story, God created man in His image, but this was not about physical appearance. It was about humanity

---

[5] James Baldwin, *I Am Not Your Negro*.

housing the very breath of God within them. When sin entered the world, that image was marred. The effect of sin was separation: separation between Creator and creation, and separation between people. Sin immediately impacted how humanity related with each other. The gospel of Christ restores the image and harmony of God in humanity. When God's people move from pain to purpose, from hostility to harmony, from divided to united, the Gospel of Christ reverberates throughout creation and in the church. The church that Christ envisioned always required humanity to be united in Him, and in turn with each other.

This book strives to empower leaders in the body of Christ to tear down the walls that hinder others of all ethnicities from leading in the multiethnic family known as the Church. It is about combating the walls in our heads that tell us only certain groups of people can lead other groups of people. It is about preparing and equipping leadership teams and denominations with helpful frameworks to empower leaders from every ethnicity. It is about making room for leaders who are ready to lead.

In writing this book, we need to answer the following question: Who are we writing to? Are we writing primarily to pastors who desire to lead multicultural churches and ministries? Is this for the denominations and sending churches that desire to make room for leaders of all ethnicities? Is this for the everyday Christian who cares about seeing healthy churches that reflect the ethnic and cultural diversity of the kingdom of God? The answer to all these questions is yes. As we worked through this book, we wrestled with what was being left out: the focus on the different challenges female pastors face when leading multicultural congregations, Hispanic and Asian leadership in the multiethnic church, and the differences between leading multiethnic churches in different parts of the world. On one hand, this book has a level of applicability to each of these areas. On the other, there is much more research that needs to be done and more books to be written before the body of Christ can better equip and empower leaders to benefit His church and His world. *Ready to Lead* is a book about Black leadership in the multiethnic church and tearing down the walls that hinder the body of Christ from benefiting from their leadership.

2

Nothing New Under the Sun

So there is nothing new under the sun.
—Ecclesiastes 1:9

Because this book addresses Black leadership in the multiethnic church, it is important to realize that the idea of Black people leading in diverse contexts is not a recent phenomenon. We saw it in the early days of our republic, even during times of slavery. During the 1700s and 1800s, many White brothers and sisters in Christ, as well as Christians from other ethnicities, were ministered to and benefited from Black pastors. For brief periods, White evangelicals encouraged converted, enslaved Christians to exercise their preaching gifts. This made Black preaching a regular part of the Baptist and Methodist communities. In some churches, Black pastors even served racially diverse congregations.[6]

In the United States, one of the first Black pastors to lead a congregation with a considerable number of Whites was Lemuel Haynes. He became the first African American ordained by an American religious body in 1785. He was also the first African American with an honorary master's degree.[7] Haynes served as pastor at the West Parish of Rutland, Vermont, for thirty years. This was unique in that it was an all-White congregation in the later

---

[6] Hatch, 106; Raboteau, 133.
[7] Anyabwile and Piper, 18.

part of the eighteenth century. Under his leadership, the church grew from forty-two members to 350.[8]

There are several other documented examples of Black preachers whose ministries crossed ethnic lines in the eighteenth and nineteenth centuries. One is Josiah Bishop, an enslaved minister who took over preaching duties in 1792 for a diverse church in Portsmouth, Virginia. It is important to remember that diversity in leadership does not mean that Blacks were treated on equal footing as White parishioners. However, Bishop's impact across ethnic lines was so great that his freedom was eventually purchased by the same congregation he pastored.[9] It is mind-blowing to me that he had to have his freedom purchased by his congregants. Because he was Black and pastoring Whites in a slave-holding state, he had to move on after a short and successful stint as pastor.[10]

A contemporary of Josiah Bishop who also ministered across ethnic lines was Andrew Bryan. He was a gifted and well-respected Black preacher who preached to both Blacks and Whites.[11] He was also part of establishing Silver Bluff, the oldest Black Baptist church in America, which started in Savannah, Georgia, in 1773. Bryan eventually took the reins of leadership after George Liele's departure to do missions work. While Bryan was loved and respected by people of all colors, his persecution was well documented. He was beaten and imprisoned for ministering the gospel, yet he continued to have an impact on both Blacks and Whites until his death in 1812.[12]

Other Black preachers ministered across the Black-White divide during the height of slavery. In 1792, a man by the name of Uncle Jack was recognized as a powerful Baptist preacher. Many Whites came to Christ under his ministry.[13] A Methodist preacher named Henry Evans also ministered to many Whites in the late 1700s. They attended his meetings in Fayetteville, North Carolina, and although he initially experienced opposition, his ministry so transcended color lines that a church was

---

[8] Anyabwile, 20.
[9] Raboteau, 134.
[10] Woodson, 55.
[11] Woodson, 47–48.
[12] Woodson, 49–52.
[13] Woodson, 55–56.

started there. While he did minister at the church, the church itself was overseen by a White minister.[14]

The early 1800s continued to produce Black preachers who led biracial congregations and ministries. In the early nineteenth century, a White Baptist church in Gloucester County, Virginia, was pastored by a Black man named William Lemon.[15] A few years later, in 1808, a free Black missionary named John Chavis started a school for children in Raleigh, North Carolina. This school ministered to Blacks and Whites until the school was shut down because John Chavis preached publicly in 1832.[16]

Nat Turner was a Black preacher in Southampton County, Virginia. Turner grew to prominence as a gifted and insightful minister. In the 1830s, he led a revolt against his White slave owners, which caused lawmakers and slave owners to worsen slavery conditions. Turner's rebellion made Whites a lot more hesitant to allow Blacks to publicly minister. Harry Hosier, also known as Black Harry, was a preacher who traveled with Francis Asbury and other well-known Christian leaders. He spoke to packed crowds of Blacks and Whites. Many people considered him one of the most gifted communicators of his day.[17]

What Do These Black Preachers Have in Common?

Each of these preachers had different stories, but they also shared similarities that enabled them to effectively minister across racial lines when our nation openly embraced racism. When we look into their lives and ministry journeys, at least three commonalities consistently emerge:

1. Exceptional Gifts: These men had exceptional ministry gifts that could not be denied, making them appear as exceptions.
2. Persecuting Circumstances: These preachers had to deal with a measure of persecution, or at least resistance.
3. Seen as Nonthreatening: They were willing to work within a racialized system in a way that was seen as non threatening to Whites.

---

[14] Woodson, 56.
[15] Raboteau, 134.
[16] Raboteau, 135.
[17] Hatch, 106.

Here are just a few pronounced examples of how these attributes were prevalent in their ministries and in their lives.

John Chavis was known to be an exceptional student and was sent to Princeton to study even as a Black man in the 1700s. In response to the ministry of this Black preacher and educator in North Carolina, a White lawyer remarked, "His English was remarkably pure, containing no Negroisms; his manner was impressive ..."[18] This could be comparable to someone today saying to a Black man, "You are amazingly articulate for a Black person." His speech was seen as acceptable because it was seen as other than Black in the eyes of this lawyer. (I have personally heard it said about me, "Don't worry, he is Black but he's good.")

Lemuel Haynes preached at a church in Connecticut. A man of repute in the community was not happy about a "Black minister" and set forth to show outright disrespect toward him. It was not until Haynes preached that this man's attitude changed. He commented, "He had not preached far when I thought I saw the whitest man I ever knew in that pulpit, and I tossed my hat under the pew."[19] For Haynes to be accepted by this man in the congregation meant he had to be seen as something other than Black. Hayne's superb oratory skill was recognized, but it was only after he was seen as the "whitest man" that he was able to get this man's respect.

Andrew Bryan, a slave converted in 1792, was whipped and imprisoned for holding meetings with Blacks without White supervision.[20] The fear was that too many Blacks attending his meetings meant a possible threat to the slave owners and their agenda. As a result, he was not free to lead his congregation without seeming to pose a threat, which led him to appear in court. Bryan's ministry gifts were seen as a liability and threat until people were confident that it was not a threat to White slave owners.[21]

The strong combination of exceptional gifts, persecuting circumstances, and being seen as non threatening, which in some cases is synonymous with resembling whiteness, enabled these Black preachers to lead diverse populations in a racist environment. These are just a few of many examples of what Black preachers of the gospel had to navigate. In certain situations,

---

[18] Woodson, 69.
[19] Woodson, 63.
[20] Hatch, 49.
[21] Hatch, 50.

some might wonder if these qualities are necessary for Black preachers to lead multiethnic communities today.

In a 2017 article responding to Blacks congregants leaving White evangelicalism, Bryan Lorrits, a Black pastor of a multiethnic church, spoke of the challenges Blacks pastors face in predominantly White churches: "I don't know y'all, but at the age of 44, and having spent over half my life as a guest in the white evangelical world, I'm tired of begging to be noticed, considered, and invited."[22] It would seem that at least some of the challenges Blacks faced in the seventeenth and eighteenth centuries still hold true for some Black pastors leading and pastoring where White people are present in abundant numbers.

Once colored talent is noticed, it is promoted and highly sought after, but at times only as entertainment. At times we still see African Americans limited to a level of entertainment even in our culture and the church—in music, preaching, or sports. It is a challenge for the minority leader to break through certain barriers unless they are very exceptional. Exceptional gifts and being a non-threatening person continue to be common ingredients that allow minority leaders to cross the threshold of multiethnic ministry.

Oddly enough, this is seen not just in pulpits but also in music ministry. There was a great wave of Christian hip-hop led by popular Christian artists from Reach Records. They exhibit an exceptional stage presence yet conservative theology. They were widely accepted in predominantly White circles. Hip-hop crossed the cultural boundaries. It was an avenue that enabled African Americans to enter predominantly, large, White events and churches. Once again, it took exceptional talent for the crossover to occur. Even in that space, however, some would later express that while they were accepted on the stage, they did not feel as accepted in the greenroom. The questions that we address throughout this book will help us wrestle with the unseen barriers and red tape that hinder minority leaders and multiethnic ministry from flourishing.

---

[22] Loritts, "More on Leaving White Evangelicalism."

Part 2

Honest Questions

Books and studies on the topic of multiethnic churches continue to give new insights on the body of Christ. Some of these insights challenge our preconceived ideas and foster growth, but all too often other discussions suggest solutions with a familiar formula: bring someone diverse on your staff, play a song that is ethnically diverse every so often, include people on stage that demonstrate diversity, and make sure all your pictures on social media reflect diversity. This is not a bad start. These considerations are important to us as we lead our churches. However, these efforts only scratch the surface. Many people have attempted these methods only to find that their church did not suddenly become multiethnic and a place of true reconciliation. Even more difficult, those that do become multiethnic are sometimes unable to withstand the forces causing division during times of intense racial tension in society.

These surface-level solutions often leave Christian leaders confused. The desire is there, the faith is there, and the ministry gifts are there. Yet there are things under the surface that stifle healthy diversity in churches and limit the pastors' ability to lead them.

Understanding the unique challenges and opportunities for Black-led multiethnic churches became such a puzzle to me that I (Brian) dedicated three years of my doctoral research to this topic. My research included a comparative analysis with ten Black pastors leading multiethnic churches and ten White pastors leading multiethnic churches. (As I mentioned before, I define multiethnic congregations as those with no more than 80 percent of one ethnicity.) Each pastor who participated in the study identified their ethnic identity.

What I found was that our White brothers and sisters who lead multiethnic churches have many of the same challenges that Black pastors have, although these challenges may show up in different forms. This stands as a stark reminder that we all share this hope to see the bride of Christ reconciled across cultural lines of division. However, there are also some key differences to recognize for Black pastors leading diverse churches.

Below is a list that formed from analyzing the survey results in my research. It reveals the most common challenges that participants faced while leading a multiethnic church:

- political challenges (how to address issues where race and politics intersect)
- leadership issues (how to lead people through ethnic tension)
- stylistic challenges (how the preaching and music are shaped by cultural differences)
- assimilation (how to go from simply meeting together to eating together)
- vision (how to set a God-given vision for a multiethnic church), financial (how finances play a role in the ethnic dynamics)
- cultural challenges (how we account for the different cultural expectations in a diverse church).

We can see the comparison between the Black participants and the White participants.

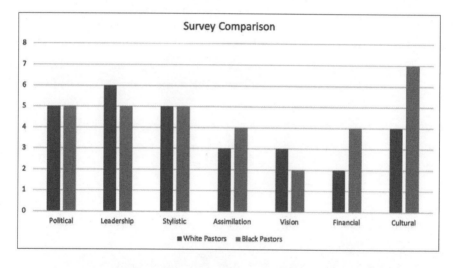

This chart shows the broad categories that the survey participants identified as challenges to leading multiethnic churches, but it does not describe how these same challenges play out differently among the pastors. I gained more insight from the interviews that accompanied my surveys, which brought up more considerations into this topic.

Before I was a researcher, I was a pastor of a multiethnic church and friend to many pastors of different ethnicities leading multiethnic churches. I find it interesting that I have heard from people representing different nations and ethnicities, and the same challenges and questions resonated with them in different contexts. The seven questions in the chapters that follow are ones that arose both from my research surveys and interviews, Chris's and my relationships with other pastors leading in multiethnic churches and ministries, and our personal experiences in multiethnic churches.

1. The Question of Credibility: Am I Enough to Lead You?
2. The Question of Culture: Do I Have to Abandon My Blackness?
3. The Question of Conscience: Can I Honestly Talk about Issues?
4. The Question of Currency: Are There Strings Attached?
5. The Question of Courage: Are We Ready to Talk?
6. The Question of Conviction: Is it Worth the Headache?
7. The Question of Collaboration: Can We Mutually Submit?

3

The Question of Credibility: Am I Enough to Lead You?

> He's pretty good for a Black pastor.
> —Anonymous

It is important to understand that leading any church, especially any multiethnic church, is difficult for pastors of any ethnicity. It is also important to recognize the leadership challenges in these spaces may look different based on the leader's ethnicity. For White pastors leading in multiethnic churches and ministries, the leadership challenge is often about sharing power. *How do I make room at the table for those who don't look like me?* I was able to witness this unique quality with Dr. Rice Broocks's leadership at my church in Tennessee in the early 2000's. He was willing, as a White pastor, to truly give away power to a Black pastor to lead Bethel, a church that became several thousand. He brought on Tim Johnson, a Black pastor who has since become a mentor and friend of mine, as one of Bethel's pastors. During that time, I witnessed our church go from a predominantly White church to a very diverse, multiethnic church, represented by many different nations. Depending on the Sunday, we might have Pastor Tim preach or we might have Dr. Rice preach. This was not a token role or window dressing on Sunday morning; Dr. Rice relinquished his power as the senior pastor and empowered Pastor Tim to become the senior pastor of the church. While this scenario is specific to Rice Broocks and Tim Johnson, it highlights an important point for our topic. In order for White pastors to lead with shared power, it often requires a willingness to sacrifice their own power, privilege, and preference. Without an intentional effort to lay the idols of power, privilege, and preference at the altar, bringing in pastors of other ethnicities often feels like tokenism.

Sharing power is sometimes a leadership obstacle for Black pastors, but the more prevalent challenge in leadership for Black pastors looks different in multiethnic spaces: it is not the issue of sharing, but the issue of credibility. *Can I prove myself to be credible enough for those who are not Black, or any other ethnic minority, to follow me?* This goes back to the example of Lemuel Haynes being perceived by another White parishioner as "the whitest man I ever knew in that pulpit" in order to gain the respect of that congregant.

What does it take to be seen as credible enough for non black people to follow a Black pastor? There is a big difference between people who are willing to listen to your sermon on a podcast and those willing to follow your leadership. One can be inspired, impressed, entertained, and even changed by the ministry of a black pastor, but yet not submitted to a Black pastor's leadership and vision. This looks like a willingness to participate and immerse into communities led by Black pastors. This point can be demonstrated in other diverse settings where Black people are in leadership roles. In an article examining Black professors on White campuses, Lorenzo Middleton found that "black educators, particularly, seem to be resigned to an atmosphere of professional and social isolation on white campuses."[23] He further elaborates on this dilemma by stating the pressure felt by some to constantly "prove" their mettle to white colleagues.[24] Leadership in general is challenging enough, but it is even more so when done with a need to prove oneself.

The pressure to prove one's value as a professor is amplified by evaluations given by students at the end of a semester. Student evaluations play a pivotal role in the hiring, promotion, range of salary, and tenure of professors at universities.[25] According to a 2009 study by Ho, Thomsen,

---

[23] Middleton.
[24] Middleton.
[25] Basow et al., 352.

and Sidanius on rating professor competence and sensitivity, women and African Americans have the greater burden to prove competence in higher-level positions.[26] An example of this is seen in an interview where host Anthony Bradley shared his reality as a Black professor: "When a black male professor stands in a room with predominantly white students … I have a 5–10 minute window on the first day of class to dispel the notions of what my students assume black men are like. If I fail in that 5–10 minute window my evaluation will be lower."[27]

One of the ways this credibility challenge presents itself in the church with Black pastors is through what I like to call the "signing-off syndrome." This means that until your theology, mettle, or leadership is signed off on by someone deemed more credible, (which, sadly, often means someone who is White), then you are not fully trusted in certain circles. I am sure this happens for younger pastors and women of any ethnicity, as well. However, this is prevalent for many Black pastors in diverse settings. I appreciate and have been blessed by many White pastors and pastors from all backgrounds, but I do not need them to validate pastors that have meant so much to me through the years.

Let me take this opportunity to say the credibility question can be a bit challenging to detect because it is not always overtly asked; in fact, I would be surprised if many people even recognize this credibility check is what they are demanding. Few, if any, Christians I know would plainly state or agree with the idea that a pastor is *less than* because of the color of their skin. I do not know of people going to church services with their arms folded, demanding proof of credibility. However, our cultural conditioning can run so deep that it must be called out so we can see ourselves.

We are naturally geared to be more comfortable in environments of sameness. When entering a different social setting, we unconsciously look for or gravitate towards people who are most like us. While experiencing the exhilaration of something new, we also have to deal with the hesitations of the unknown. I have had several conversations with some of our White congregants who attended our church in the smaller, and less diverse state. When they entered the church, they felt older, and whiter than ever before. They commented that they looked for other white people, and gray hair.

---

[26] Basow et al., 354.
[27] Keller et al., sec.17 minutes in.

Now many of these individuals have become faithful members of our congregation for many years, and have advocated for racial reconciliation in many different contexts across our country. Even with their background, seeing someone like them gave our young developing church some credibility. The question of credibility naturally exists in us, but it is even greater when the leadership does not look like you.

As a Black man raised in America, it was impossible for me to grow up without having people of other ethnicities in positions of authority over me. I experienced it in school growing up with teachers and principals. I had coaches who were White, I had employers who were White, and it never was a thing. As I talked with some of my White friends, including some congregants in the church I lead, they shared that they grew up in environments that did not require them to have anyone other than a White person in authority over them their entire lives. It was not as though they outright rejected the idea of a Black person in authority; it was just that it was never a reality they lived in. It often becomes difficult for some of our White brothers and sisters to understand why they struggle to feel at home in a church with a Black pastor when they appreciate the music, preaching, and so many other aspects of the church. Perhaps under the surface is the question of credibility.

As we deal with the question of credibility stemming from people's perspectives from the outside, we must also address the idea of metaperception that comes from inside of us. Metaperception is how you perceive other people are perceiving you. To some degree, we all live with an awareness of how we are seen by others. But for Black pastors, there is a strong awareness of how you are negatively perceived, especially in diverse environments where White people are present in large numbers. Most people carry some level of inaccurate metaperceptions, and if you are in environments where you constantly have to prove yourself you can easily allow your leadership and preaching to be shaped by the need to seem credible. If I believe that I am always seen as *less than*, it may cause me to go to extreme lengths to show I am worthy to be taken seriously.

I remember talking with fellow Black pastors and leaders about how we are perceived by non-Blacks as a leader. Our fellow White pastors can get away with dressing in jeans and sandals, but we better make sure we have something presentable on at all times if we want to be credible with certain audiences. We cannot use slang in our preaching and communication lest we come across as unprofessional and uneducated. These are some examples of how the question of credibility comes into play for Black pastors in leadership.

This is a good place for me to mention the relationships that have formed among our staff at Every Nation Cincinnati Church, particularly the relationship that has formed between my associate pastor and me. A big reason for the diversity we have seen in our church is due to Dr. Steve Robinson. He is a White man, a medical doctor. He is older than I am. We work as a team, and although he works full time at the hospital, he carries great influence in our church, as well. When we go into meetings and rooms with other leaders and people in the community, he introduces me as his pastor. At times, I can sense the surprise from people when they learn who the lead pastor is. However, his willing acknowledgment of my role in his life has been necessary to establish credibility for some. I am not sure that this was his purpose; he was just stating the reality. My current staff members are White, Black, Latino, and Filipino. They call me pastor and I consider it a joy to serve them as their leader. I am reminded on multiple occasions that what may be normal for us is not necessarily normal for everybody.

Tips for Black Pastors

There are several tips I could offer that may help you seem more credible to others. Always dress professionally, get more degrees so that you can be respected more, eliminate any slang from your preaching, be well versed in code switching, and be sure to quote and reference popular White theologians whenever you speak or write. While these may be helpful tips, they can also add an even bigger problem. If you spend more time thinking about who you think people want you to be rather than thinking about who God made you to be, you will never be the best pastor your church needs, and you will probably feel burned out from all that pressure.

Here are a few things to keep in mind as we wrestle through the credibility question.

- **Be aware.** There are unique hurdles that people have in their minds when it comes to Black pastors and pastors in general.

Before we become too offended at this idea, remember we all carry certain biases that we may not even be aware of. Being aware of how you can be perceived is not the same as capitulating to an image people want you to fall into.
- **Be grateful.** I realize that there are Black pastors who have gone before me who have had to endure a lot just to be seen as credible enough to lead. I, along with many pastors in my generation, as well as younger pastors, stand on their shoulders. Thank God for them.
- **Be consistent.** It may take time for people to appreciate who you are and what you bring to the table. Remember, it was God who called you. Be faithful and consistent in what He has called you to do, "knowing that your labor is not in vain" (1 Corinthians 15:58).

Tips for Leaders Supporting Black Pastors

Earlier I mentioned our associate pastor, Steve Robinson. He was willing to put himself under the leadership of a Black pastor. I think more of this is needed. Whether you are another pastor in a city with other Black pastors or on staff with a Black pastor, willingly find ways to actively support the leadership of pastors who are godly and gifted, but may not look like you. Be careful that this kind of submission is not one where you submit as long as you are never challenged or asked to feel uncomfortable. This does not have to diminish your leadership, but it can strengthen a Black pastor's leadership in some cases.

Tips for Congregants of Black Pastors

For those who are congregants of multiethnic churches, the question for you is why? What moved you to attend? Did you get saved in that church? Did you appreciate the preaching or the community that was formed? There is a reason why you attended, and it is important that you think about that from time to time. At some point, there was something that caused you to want to be a part of the church this pastor leads. Remember, God did not draw you to that popular preacher's church that you listen to from time to time on the internet. God did not call you to the pastor's church that sounds like what you heard growing up. He called you to be a part of the church that your pastor is leading. Appreciate who your pastor is—the strengths and the weaknesses. Here are some other considerations as you show support to your pastor.

Find ways to show honor. Romans 12:10 says: "Be devoted to one another in brotherly love; give preference to one another in honor." You could also say, "Outdo one another in showing honor." I understand the problem that can come with pastor worship that unfortunately has been seen in many churches. There have been times when we as pastors have allowed ourselves to be treated as superstars, or worse, unrivaled dictators. That is not what this verse in Romans means. Honor is not a bad word; it is a way of showing brotherly love and being devoted to one another.

Another way to view honor is expressed loyalty. A good friend and mentor of mine talks about the value of expressed loyalty. Loyalty should be heard, seen, and felt. This means expressing words of appreciation and affirmation verbally, and with presence. Expressed loyalty causes one to not allow slander, or unnecessary scrutiny to go unconfronted. Expressed loyalty is not silent or hidden. It is intentional and edifying. This encourages the leader, and reminds others why they have chosen to be part of the church and this pastor's leadership.

How you refer to your pastor matters. I realize that some of this is cultural, and this needs to be kept in mind. For predominantly Black churches, there is a tendency to use titles when speaking to pastors or about them. At many of the predominantly White churches it seems more normal to hear pastors called by their first names. This often goes beyond the church setting. I could never imagine calling my mother or father-in-law by their first names, but that seems fairly normal for many of my White brothers and sisters. So it only makes sense that in many multiethnic churches, mine included, most White congregants call their pastors by their first names.

This is rarer with Black congregants I have come in contact with. I believe this is due to several factors. It is not just that Black pastors have some deep insecurity that needs to be stroked by getting a title, although I'm sure there are some exceptions to this rule. Imagine living in a world where you are degraded, called out of your name, even being called a boy as a grown man. Now what is the one institution outside the home where Black people were able to truly experience an environment where we were honored and respected? The church. James is not just James, he is Brother James. Betty is not just Betty, she is Sister Betty or even Aunt Betty, though there is no blood relationship. The pastor is not just Henry, he is Reverend Henry Jones.

This does not mean that the answer is to start calling your pastor by every title you can think up. It means be mindful of how you use or don't use titles, and do not assume a casualness with your pastor outside of the relationship. Most people would not walk in the doctor's office and call their doctor by their first name until a relationship is established, but outside of the doctor's office it may be more casual.

Discussion Questions for Leadership Teams

> How are titles utilized within your context?
> How is power shared within your leadership team?
> What makes a leader worth following?
> Where have my biases been revealed because of this chapter?
> Where have my fears been revealed because of this chapter?

4

The Question of Culture: Do I Have to Abandon My Blackness?

I will give thanks to You, for I am fearfully and wonderfully made; wonderful are Your works, and my soul knows it very well.
(Psalm 139:14)

I have found that not every Black pastor jumps with excitement at the idea of a multiethnic church. For many, this push for diversity, whether intentionally or unintentionally, means Black people have to strip themselves of any cultural vestiges to make ourselves less threatening and more palatable for other groups. I realize how silly abandoning my Blackness as a question may seem, since intrinsically we are who we are. However, what this question really asks is how much of my Blackness is allowed to show for non-Blacks to still feel included in my congregation.

There seems to be a misunderstanding of contextualization in our contemporary church world. Contextualization in its pure form means the language and other practices that are acceptable and valid in church. Brian Loritts did an excellent job shedding light on the tension that comes with contextualizing church culture. He illuminated a W.E.B. Du Bois quote about the strife that the African American lives in:

> It is a peculiar sensation, this double-consciousness, this sense of always looking at one's self through the eyes of others, of measuring one's soul by the tape of a world that looks on in amused contempt and pity. One ever feels his two-ness,—an American, a Negro; two souls, two thoughts, two unreconciled strivings; two warring ideals in one dark body, whose dogged strength alone keeps it from being torn asunder. The history of the American Negro is the history of this strife,—this longing to attain self-conscious manhood, to merge his double self into a better and truer self.[28]

Contextualization should still leave room for celebrations, and we should celebrate things that are different instead of eliminating things that are different. A true multiethnic church is supposed to show a full expression of the gifts of the Spirit and how they are expressed through different cultures; if there is a dominant culture, it is just a one-way street. We have to accept that because there are multiple cultures represented, there won't be a type of culture that applies to all multiethnic churches. Each church has an opportunity to develop its own unique culture. We must remember that culture is the product of a people group forming into a community, not simply a community that is forming people. All multiethnic churches will not look or sound the same, but they will reveal a fuller example of the gospel that goes beyond human divisions and schisms.

What I (Chris) want to advocate for is a church discovery process as people from different backgrounds come together. A church discovery process could look like the intentional efforts that model Acts 2:44-47 where people come together to discuss the word of God and share a meal. This can be in a home, another common grounds place, or even a regularly scheduled fellowship at the church. These moments give opportunity for people to have deep and meaningful, none reactionary conversations about matters where they differ, or may not be as knowledgeable. I have found that the combination of healthy bible teaching and fellowship among believers expedite the deepening of relationships. Even though I have over 50 percent Caucasians in my congregation, I don't want them to simply

---

[28] Loritts, 36–37

assimilate to my traditional Black and *bapticostal* approach to church and ministry. I want us to add to one another rather than take away from one another. In a healthy church context, there should be an outpouring of hospitality that ushers in a freedom to worship and a feeling of being welcomed. One of our house habits at our church is: "There is no meeting, if there is no eating." This house habit emphasizes quality relationship building when we gather. Unity does not mean uniformity. We must learn to be unified and diversified at the same time. Unity is a uniquely woven cloth of people who celebrate the Savior.

Sociologist Curtis DeYoung suggests in his book *United by Faith* three different types of multiethnic churches: The most common form of these three is the assimilated multicultural congregation.[29] Churches that build multicultural and multiethnic congregations through assimilation are ones that build primarily according to one dominant ethnic culture; those in the minority ethnic cultures simply adapt and assimilate into the dominant culture.[30] Any ethnicity can be represented as the dominant culture and any ethnicity can find itself adjusting to the dominant culture. For instance, White people can find themselves assimilating into a church culture that is primarily led and attended by Black congregants, and Black people can find themselves assimilating into a church that is primarily led by Asians.[31]

In Kevin Gushiken's article "Paulo Freire and His Contribution to Multiethnic Churches," he makes it clear he believes that this assimilated form is the most common form of multiethnic church. He observed that in most cases, these churches are diverse in terms of those who attend, but homogeneous in practice, as they "operate based on the traditions and perspectives of the dominant ethnic group."[32] In an ethnographic study of a diverse church in downtown Chicago, Jessica Barron unveiled a mindset that can easily develop in an assimilated church culture. Although church members and staff described themselves as diverse, there were no non-White staff members, the musical styles lacked diversity outside of the typical White Protestant evangelical music, the sermons never mentioned

---

[29] DeYoung et al., 165.
[30] DeYoung et al., 165.
[31] DeYoung et al., 166–167.
[32] Gushiken, 122.

diversity, and there was no programming committed to integration or diversity.[33] In fact, some African Americans within the congregation felt the resistance when desiring more positions of leadership within the church. As one Black attender said, "It's like Michigan Avenue ... you [Black men] can buy but you can't own. It's the same thing here at Downtown Church."[34]

Assimilation is one of the major challenges in multicultural churches led by pastors of all ethnicities. The majority culture may not see color, but they tend to keep their culture intact while minority cultures lose theirs in the community. Genesis 1:26 says: "Let Us make man in Our image, according to Our likeness ..." When faith communities nullify the distinctiveness of a culture, we fail to see God's image and manifold wisdom reflected fully among His people. Although this challenge manifests itself in many forms, the most prevalent battlefield for this question of culture is visible with the music and preaching delivery.

It's worth mentioning here that there is an inherent danger in using such broad strokes to describe the Black church or even the Black experience as a whole. As Jared Alcantara warns, "The temptation is to slip into totalizing, essentialist, and reductive statements about what all African Americans encounter or what all African Americans face."[35] It is important to note that in looking at these distinct characteristics of preaching and music, there are many varying expressions found within the Black church, and some Black churches and denominations have almost as many differences as similarities. In Howell's and Paris's work on anthropology, they warned that culture is dynamic and using an "ethnic fair" approach to culture can fail to account for the richness within culture itself. An oversimplified approach to culture can imply that people belong to one culture when indeed people and organizations are influenced by many different cultures.[36] Yet even with these distinctive attributes between Blacks and the congregations that they lead, one common thread that the Black church has is shared experience, including a history of oppression in this nation.[37]

---

[33] Barron, 26.
[34] Barron 27.
[35] Alcántara, 160.
[36] Howell and Paris, 27.
[37] Usry and Keener, 17.

Many books have addressed the question of music and preaching as it relates to multiethnic churches: *How do we find musicians who can play across diverse genres of music?* Many Black pastors of multiethnic churches have lamented the fact that gospel-sounding music, a genre closely associated with Black church, is either nonexistent or so rare that it is identified as a foreign phenomenon reserved for special occasions and outside of the normal flow of the gathered church. I don't think this is the result of overt racism or bigotry, but rather ethnocentrism. This way of thinking does not say that everyone else is wrong and I am right; it says everything else is foreign and my culture is normal. For example, imagine there were three people who grew up going to church: an African American young man grew up in a predominately Black church in a predominately Black neighborhood, a Latina woman grew up in a predominately Hispanic church in a thriving metropolitan area in a major city, and a White man grew up in a predominately White suburban church. They all grow up and go to the same multiethnic church as young adults. Who do you think would have to culturally adjust the most in order to be a part of this church? Who would have to adjust the least? Typically, the people who grow up in predominantly White churches have to adjust the least in multiethnic churches when it comes to style of music, dress code, preaching style, etc.

Korie Edwards, a sociologist from Ohio State who has contributed greatly to the understanding of race and the church in America, provided context in her research. In 1998, 20 percent of church attendees were in all-White congregations, and by 2006–07 that number dropped to 14 percent. However, churches that have been predominantly African American, Hispanic, or Asian have seen no change in the percentage of attendees over the same period of time. This means that churches that have been predominantly White are becoming more diverse and seems to suggest that the traction we are seeing in the multiethnic movement is about non-White groups assimilating into the White culture.[38]

There are several reasons that may contribute to this reality that White congregants are not coming into Black churches in large part. It is possible for many White people to grow up in the United States and never be in situations where they are the minority or have to assimilate into a predominant culture other than their own. This will not be the case in

---

[38] Edwards et al., 215.

the future as demographic shifts continue to take place by 2050. Because White people are not accustomed to being in the minority, my guess is that they are less likely to move to a church where they are not the majority culture. However, because many other ethnic groups in the United States are used to being in the minority, it is easier for them to adjust to other dominant cultures. Honestly, I have seen ministries and churches that have been predominantly White transition to become multiethnic, but there are not many examples of transitions taking place in the opposite direction.

During my time in Orlando, a few years before planting my own church in Cincinnati, I served as a pastor on staff and focused a lot on ministering to college students. Through a couple of connections, I was put in contact with some students at the University of Central Florida. I was invited to speak to this group and then asked to come back again. After a few times of going to this group, many people, myself included, sensed that God was building a deeper connection. This group was predominately made up of Black students, representing different cultures such as Haitian, Jamaican, Nigerian, and African American. This Christian ministry was uniquely started to provide a place for Black students to worship together on a predominately White campus. While I appreciated the original reason for the formation of this group, I operated with a conviction that God wanted us to reach people from all nations and ethnicities. This was a wonderful and challenging undertaking.

I recently had a chance to talk with a friend of mine who was a student during these years, and he gave me perspective on what many of our Black student population felt in our ministry during that time. "We highlighted the people reaching outside of the Black population, but in so doing we wore it as a badge of honor to drop our Blackness in order to reach them … the question that we wrestled with was 'Is Black wrong?'" The teaching from our senior pastor, and later myself as well, opened the door for people to be comfortable with who they were and unapologetic about their Blackness while still opening the door for other groups to come be a part.

One aspect of the ministry that was there before I arrived was their step team. This was no ordinary step team; they could compete with the best of the best. A step team, closely associated with historically Black fraternities and sororities, is a group of people who participate in a coordinated dance that combines stomping, rhythm, and coordinated movement. I can remember going with our students to our campus conference where they were going to be ministering through stepping. Again, this form of ministry has been used by people of all ethnicities, but it is undeniably Black in its roots. It was new to the group gathered at the conference we were ministering to in North Carolina, but it was also embraced. I was unsure of how this form of worship would be received, but I was pleasantly surprised. If churches and ministries are going to be truly diverse, then there must be a willingness to embrace different cultural expressions in their services and other worship experiences.

In a case study of a multiethnic church, sociologist Korie Edwards highlighted the challenges of the Black pastor in connecting to Blacks and Whites: "Whites appreciated him for what many African-Americans did not, his intellectual religious orientation. He emphasized understanding spiritual things more than experiencing them. Yet, he was also caught between two worlds. He was not fully embraced by either African Americans or Whites." Edwards went on to explain the tension, saying that Blacks felt frustration at the lack of bringing more of the African American religious culture to church. Whites were accepting as long as "those parts of his identity that were particular to his Black experience remained concealed."[39] This act of walking a fine line causes many Black people, and leaders especially, to assimilate into a system and culture that is foreign to their Black heritage in churches that are moving toward diversity. Edwards makes this observation based on a 2008 study:

> Multiracial congregations, when compared with both predominantly white congregations and congregations of color, are more inclined to participate in the kinds of religious and extra religious practices in which predominantly white churches participate. Situating her findings in critical whiteness theory, Edwards (2008b) argues that because whites are accustomed to being culturally normative and structurally privileged and are unused to addressing issues of race, multiracial congregations will need to minimize racial conflict and primarily address the preferences and desires of whites if they are to keep whites attending.[40]

---

[39] Edwards, *Elusive Dream*, 66.
[40] Edwards et al, Race, Religious Organizations, and Integration, 221

I also want to address and challenge worship leaders and music directors. During my research, I conducted an interview with a Black pastor of a multiethnic church who pointed out the challenge of diverse worship in the church. He noticed, as have many others, that the default seems to always be white contemporary worship. If the multiethnic church where you lead only sings songs that are more normative in White culture, then give alternatives. Challenge your praise teams and band members to move beyond their comfort zone and give them grace to grow in the process.

Let me say that we as a church do not always get this perfect; in fact, many days we find ourselves asking how we can do this better as it relates to music. One of the things I appreciate from our worship leader and the team as a whole, besides their musical skills and knowledge, is their willingness to keep coming to the table to listen and learn. There was a time when one of our worship leaders, who happens to be White, sang a throwback song from gospel artist Eddie James and received an interesting response. At the end of service, our worship singer was told, "You have no business singing that song. You do not understand the struggle that they went through to write it." Fortunately, it did not cause this singer to quit our worship team, but it was a reminder of the musical minefields that can erupt in a multiethnic environment. Some of my Black brothers and sisters may find it offensive for White people to sing songs attributed to Black people and the Black struggle. People are entitled to their viewpoints on this. I saw this as a step in the direction of us growing in our cultural diversity as a church.

This problem of diversifying song choice is often reinforced by Christian radio stations. On multiple occasions I have heard pastors looking to popular songs on Christian radio as the guideline of what gets played in church services. This is an understandable strategy since familiarity often breeds participation as it relates to worship. The problem is that radio stations often lack diversity in their song selection. Admittedly, I have never worked in radio and may not fully understand the reasons for these decisions being made, but too few Christian radio stations incorporate a diverse sound that appeals to the multiethnic community called the church. We are often left with the choice between the Black gospel station and the White contemporary gospel station.

It is important to understand how blurred musical and cultural lines are and will progressively become. Black music and White music, and gospel music and contemporary Christian music, are becoming less distinguishable. Many artists and groups such as Todd Dulaney, Maverick City, and Every Nation Music are finding ways to integrate diverse cultural styles within their music. Our hope is that we will continue to see musical creativity grow in a way that celebrates several cultural styles while at the same time creating new ones.

The challenge in the church is not just for those singing and playing instruments, it is also for those pastors preaching in the pulpit. I grew up in a church where I heard great Black preaching and I heard many different styles within the Black church. When asked about the differences between Black churches and White churches, Claude Alexander responded by saying that Black preaching deals a lot with the immanence of God, which is in contrast to a more common approach in White churches of dealing with the transcendence of God. Both Black and White churches would affirm both the transcendence and immanence of God, but the preaching in Black churches tends to emphasize the presence of God in everyday life.[41] This often leads to an emotive style of preaching. It is important that we resist the temptation to make emotional preaching and theologically sound preaching mutually exclusive.

An example that comes to my mind is my good friend and coauthor Pastor Chris Johnson. He leads a growing multiethnic church in Harrisonburg, Virginia, and it is one of the most ethnically diverse churches I know. He is not only a good friend and a great pastor, but one of the best preachers around. Between his cultural references in preaching, his high energy and emotive style, and even use of vernacular, he is unapologetically Black in his delivery and style. He breaks the false idea that you have to preach a certain way as a Black pastor to attract non-Black congregants. When visiting his church as a guest preacher, I asked one of the young White men who was heavily involved in their ministry about what he loved about his church and his pastor. His response was so refreshing to hear: "I just like the fact that he is authentic. He doesn't apologize for who he is, and I appreciate that."

---

[41] Alexander and Anderson.

Who Hears the Black Voice, and When Is It Appropriate?

I often stand in front of diverse groups of people and ask this question: "What is one of the most iconic and memorable speeches you have heard?" The most common answer to that question is Rev. Dr. Martin Luther King Jr.'s "I Have a Dream" speech given on August 28, 1963, in Washington, D.C., at the Lincoln Memorial. Dr. King methodically used the traditional African American homiletic: "Start slow, stay low, rise higher, catch fire, sit in the storm." This approach is one that has been used in African American preaching for years. It captures tension, pain, poetry, inspiration, and celebration. Dr. King, on one the largest platforms of American history, pierced the crowd with the beauty and power of the Black voice.

As with all cultures and ethnic groups, I believe that they each represent a unique heavenly pitch and perspective. God communicates uniquely through all. Specifically as an African American (Black) man, I will speak from this perspective. The Black voice is a prophetic instrument meant to captivate and catapult people to action with one of the mightiest virtues—*hope*! Inspiration, perseverance, and hope are often embedded in the Black voice due to the nuance of pain and beauty of our history.

When the Black mind and body were attacked in slavery, the voice still rose. Negro spirituals, homilies, poetry, and a galvanized community began to emerge. The tenor of the Black voice has been forged with a combination of affliction and art and has a natural inclination toward spirited expression. The pressure, pain, and pathway of the Black voice has now yielded a prophetic edge that can't be muted. Due to the embedded sharpness and power of the Black voice, it must be handled with great responsibility, humility, and education. Not simply academic education as we have known it, but cultural education as well. I truly believe the Black voice is a meeting ground for psychological, sociological, and theological uniqueness. This is seen and heard in speaking and singing. The Black voice produced spirituals when the pain in their bodies was overcome by the hope in their hearts. The Black preaching voice inspired hope and longing for freedom and justice from the plantation to present time.

I am an unapologetic advocate for different preaching styles. I believe the action of preaching has often been degraded in contemporary church. You will hear people describe the preaching moment in church as a "talk" or "speech". Preaching is much more than a talk or a speech. Preaching is divinely inspired communication that is grounded in the word of God with the purposes of revealing God's will and calling people to surrender to the Almighty God. The beauty of black preaching has often been spoken about as being too showy, or performance based rather than EXCELLENCE. I am not simply talking about the performance of preaching, but the power that propels the performance. If the black voice is forced to assimilate the church will sideline one of its greatest and unique gifts.

Tips for Black Pastors

Do not feel guilty about considering other people. Philippians 2:3–4 says: "Do nothing from selfishness or empty conceit, but with humility of mind let each of you consider one another as more important than himself." Considering different people groups when selecting worship music or programs to implement is important. However, remember that God called you to be the pastor. The best version of yourself to offer your church is the most authentic version of who God has made you to be.

Open the door for other people inside and outside your church staff to bring diversity to your congregation by incorporating different preaching styles. This is why it is important to not only strive for a multiethnic church, but a multiethnic life. I have friends who reflect different ethnicities and different styles of preaching, but we share a commitment to the gospel. There are also people on our staff who can bring a diverse feel to our worship experiences and preaching. It is valuable for my church to hear from other pastors and voices that are different from mine.

Challenge your worship team and choirs to be willing to expand musically. Be patient with them, but challenge them nonetheless. You may have to bring other people onto your team who can help bring that musical diversity. Pray that God will show you the talent that is already in your church. It is likely that there are people within your congregation with gifts that are waiting to be activated. If they think there is no room for different styles and gifts than what they hear on a Sunday morning, they may simply sit in the back and sit on their gift. If your music team is not presenting the diversity that you believe God desires for your church, then graciously make it known.

Tips for Leaders Supporting Black Pastors

If you are a leader on staff at a multiethnic church, or any church for that matter, you can help be a steward of the culture. Pay attention to the music, preaching, and programming within the church. Be willing to be honest about what is there and what is missing. Encourage adjustments, and when pushback comes—and it usually does—stand with your pastor in taking ownership of bringing in new expressions of worship. Don't allow them to take all the flack alone when someone is not happy about a change that has taken place.

Tips for Congregants of Black Pastors

My hope for congregants in our church is that they do not simply assimilate into the cultural norms, but that they bring the uniqueness of their cultures and talents into the community. Here's what I have noticed. When someone comes to our church from a predominantly Black church, they are typically in a suit or dress. By the third or fourth week of attending, that suit becomes a pair of slacks and a nice shirt. That is fine if that is what someone desires to do, but please do not stop wearing the suit in order to fit into our culture; our community needs to be shaped by you as much as you are being shaped by it.

Here's another example. I was asked if it was OK for someone to say amen out loud when I preached. When someone comes to a church that is diverse, it can become difficult to navigate what is culturally acceptable in that moment. If everyone is fairly quiet and someone calls out "amen," it could seem inappropriate. I actually appreciate a little talk back during the sermon at appropriate times. However, this congregant needed to know that it was OK to do so. We need to be considerate of others in whatever cultural expressions we use in worship, but please do not hide who you are in order to fit in.

I also want to encourage you to be open to other forms of expression in worship and programming. If every worship song is sung in your favorite style of music, then that may mean something is wrong. It means that someone who doesn't like your style is constantly adjusting to people who like what you like. Stay open to new forms of worship and do not reject it just because it is new. This is a matter of being spiritually hospitable without compromising excellence and expression.

Discussion Questions

What would you consider your style of music at your church?

What aspects of your worship experience are based on culture and based on scriptural conviction?

What preachers do you admire and why?

What cultural barriers do people in your church have to overcome to attend?

What biases did this chapter reveal?

What fears did this chapter reveal?

5

The Question of Conscience: Can I Honestly Talk about Issues?

> People wonder, "Is he woke or just a new slave?"
> Old religion, he just covered it with new chains
> Trappin' out the church, he ain't really fake
> He divisive, he don't rep the King, he just want the fame
> Aw man, now they actin' like I'm suddenly political
> Told me shut my mouth and get my checks from Evangelicals.
> —From Lecrae's song "Facts"

As I was researching the challenge pastors face leading multiethnic churches, a recurring issue that came up for both Black and White pastors was how to handle politically and racially charged issues. Nobody I know leading a multiethnic church wants to willingly cause division, and many topics surrounding politics and policy are like powder kegs waiting to go off. This is especially true for Black pastors who often feel as if they are one misunderstood sermon or social media post away from running off congregants who fear their pastor is too empathetic to Black people's issues at the expense of the greater community.

In rapper Lecrae's case, this challenge was reflected in the lyrics above. For many years, he has been loved by many Evangelicals for his

Christ-centered and hard-hitting lyrics and beats. Many churches consisting of many ethnicities bought and promoted his music, brought him to their cities to put on Christian concerts for their youth, and supported his work in many other ways. Yet when Lecrae, a Black artist, began addressing issues that pertained to the Black community, he received a lot of backlash from the same Christian community that once supported him. He lost many fans.

Something funny happens when ethnic sensibilities get touched in a way that causes a visceral reaction. This can be illustrated by the reactions Jesus experienced early in His public ministry. Jesus was in His hometown of Nazareth, and He went into the synagogue as usual. But this time, something was different. He read from the prophet Isaiah: "The Spirit of the Lord is upon Me, because He anointed Me to preach the gospel to the poor. He has sent Me to proclaim release to the captives, and recovery of sight to the blind, to set free those who are oppressed, to proclaim the favorable year of the Lord" (Luke 4:18–9). After closing the book, Jesus went on to say: "Today this Scripture has been fulfilled in your hearing" (Luke 4:21). Notice the response in the very next verse, "And all were speaking well of Him, and wondering at the gracious words which were falling from His lips ..." All were speaking well of Jesus.

Let's be honest, this is where most preachers desire to live in their ministries; it feels good to have people speak well of us. You are loved by the people, you have a platform, and you are still preaching scripture. If Jesus had just left it there, things would have been fine. However, Jesus was not done yet: "Truly I say to you, no prophet is welcome in his hometown. But I say to you in truth, there were many widows in Israel in the days of Elijah, when the sky was shut up for three years and six months, when a great famine came over all the land; and yet Elijah was sent to none of them, but only to Zarephath, in the land of Sidon, to a woman who was a widow. And there were many lepers in Israel in the time of Elisha the prophet; and none of them was cleansed, but only Naaman the Syrian" (Luke 4:24–27).

Keep in mind, Jesus is addressing Jews and He is speaking of God bypassing them to heal a Gentile. The response after this was much different than the earlier reaction: "And all the people in the synagogue were filled with rage as they heard these things; and they got up and drove

Him out of the city, and led Him to the brow of the hill on which their city had been built, in order to throw Him down the cliff" (Luke 4:28–29). They went from speaking well of Jesus to wanting to kill Him. It was not because Jesus preached scripture; it was when Jesus had the audacity to preach scripture in a way that messed with their ethnic sensibilities. You can speak on a lot of topics in the church, even some controversial ones, but I dare say when a pastor of a multiethnic church, especially a Black pastor, messes with ethnic biases and prejudices, then that pastor may need to avoid going near any cliffs.

I believe we must clarify our goals and intentions when it comes to speaking on politically and racially charged concerns related to justice. Few people I have come across push back on anything that speaks to our need for unity in the body of Christ. However, dealing with unity means we also have to deal with matters that hinder our unity, mainly questions of justice, inequalities, and inequities. I want to submit three layers of addressing justice that are not new ideas, but newly packaged in a way that may be helpful to some: acknowledgment, accountability, and advocacy for restorative steps to make things right, including creative restitution, policy advocacy, and giving voice to marginalized populations. As pastors, we can help lead our faith communities in being voices for the marginalized, voices of conscience for our community, and at times, voices of reason.

Acknowledgment

The first desired goal when seeking justice is to acknowledge the sin. Proverbs 28:13 tells us that "He who conceals his transgressions will not prosper, but he who confesses and forsakes them will find compassion." Where we fail to acknowledge sin, we often fail to forsake it. We know this to be true in personal relationships. If I have done something wrong to another person, there should be an admission of wrongdoing if I have any hope of reconciliation. Downplaying the transgression or giving caveats and disclaimers is not the type of acknowledgment that is needed. Saying, "I'm sorry that I stole your laptop, but you shouldn't have left it out" is not a step toward reconciliation.

Now, if the need for acknowledgment of wrong is true for our personal relationships, it is also true for past offenses that have happened with groups of people in our nation. Issues of justice always seem easier to address when looking outside of one's own cultural context. Since I live in the United States, it often seems easier for believers to speak boldly about the injustices of the caste systems in India or the atrocities of the Holocaust and downplay the problems in our own backyard. Here is what I mean in an example of dismissive acknowledgment: "Yes, slavery happened, but it was a long time ago; why is it still a big deal?" We must recognize what injustice looks like in our own backyard and speak to it with courage and clarity. Our voice from the pulpit can help educate and bring awareness to the realities of our history and our present.

Black leaders face a fine line when addressing issues of race and justice while leading non-Black people. Looking at the election and presidency of Obama helps to put this reality into focus. Researchers Niambi Carter and Pearl Dowe argue that "[in] order for whites, even self-identified liberals, to feel secure about voting for Obama, they needed to know he would not betray their interests in favor of the interests of black people." They claim that Obama, a biracial man who strongly identifies with the Black identity, was able to lead at such a level in a major multiethnic environment because of "racial exceptionalism."[42]

Racial exceptionalism in President Obama's ascendancy involved affirming his Blackness and building solidarity with Blacks while universalizing his Blackness to appeal to Whites.[43] It is when Whites are assured that Black politicians do not threaten their interests that their posture toward them changes.[44] Obama had to navigate those challenges in his first election of 2008 while still overcoming the accusation of overlooking the needs and concerns of the Black community.[45] I know this tug personally, though of course from a different vocation and scale. How do you address the needs of the Black community and acknowledge the injustices within our community while still showing the other ethnicities in the church that you embrace them, too?

Obama had to learn the balancing act of identifying with his Blackness and appealing to the larger community in his early politics in Chicago.

---

[42] Carter and Dowe, 106.
[43] Carter and Dowe, 106.
[44] Carter and Dowe, 108.
[45] Carter and Dowe, 109; Terry 48–49.

Obama not only had backgrounds in Kansas and Hawaii, but he was also an Ivy League graduate. Again, this speaks to his "exceptionalism." In a rather crass statement, researcher Coates contrasts how Obama faced challenges different than Donald Trump in being elected: "To secure the White House, Obama needed to be a Harvard-trained lawyer with a decade of political experience and an incredible gift for speaking to cross sections of the country; Donald Trump needed only money and white bluster."[46]

One major strategy employed by Obama during his presidential campaign was deracialization. The theory of deracialization, brought to the spotlight by McCormick and Johnson, "argues that for black candidates seeking national leadership positions, it is prudent to forgo explicitly racial language to appeal to a wider array of voters, generally the white majority."[47] Even after Obama's election, there were times when he received backlash from even a hint of racial overtone. When he commented in July 2009 on Black Harvard professor Henry Louis Gates being arrested in his own home, he mentioned that the police "acted stupidly." As a result of this statement a third of Whites felt less favorably toward Obama.[48]

While this approach of ignoring the language of race helped with White voters, it did not always strengthen Obama's connection to the Black community, which often desired more agenda items that spoke to Black issues.[49] To this charge, President Obama responded in a 2010 edition of *Black Enterprise* that "He is not the president of Black America."[50] Other Black voices such as Britney Cooper, a professor at Rutgers, challenged Obama and other Black leaders' respectability politics. She wrote in an article, "Moderate Black people—Barack Obama included—continue to believe that the way to bring white people into the anti-racist fold is by conceding some ground in order to gain more ground."[51] Obama has had to learn how to talk about race in a way that does not "raise the ire" of Whites.[52] This has been a challenge of Blacks in leadership: creating an

---

[46] Coates 56, 66.
[47] Carter and Dowe,108.
[48] Coates, 63.
[49] Carter and Dowe, 109; Terry, 48.
[50] Terry 49.
[51] Cooper)
[52] Dyson, 5

environment that does not awaken the anger or suspicion of Whites in their contingency. Much like Andrew Bryan in the 1790s, Black leaders have often felt the need to appear non-threatening to the majority culture.

Here's where I have some confession to do. I fell into this way of thinking at times early in my pastoring as well. There were times when I was overly aware of the anger and suspicion of Whites surrounding really sensitive issues, both those in my own church and those that I am in relationship with outside of my church. My personal wiring leans toward harmony, and for that I do not apologize. I want people to get along and love each other well. (Let's just get along and reach the nations for Jesus!) This reticence to speak out has been reinforced by incidents that caused strong reactions from my brothers and sisters in Christ who did not look like me. I have seen my wife be misunderstood for simply liking a comment associated with Black Lives Matter. I have experienced times when my actions were misunderstood no matter how much of an explanation I attempted to provide.

At times as a new pastor, I was tempted to avoid the pressure of leading decisively through complex times in a multiethnic context by appealing to the goal of unity. I am grateful for my Black brothers and sisters who continually have hung in there with me as I was figuring all of this out (by the way, it is not all figured out yet). However, there were hours and hours of conversations with people who were frustrated that I did not speak up more from the pulpit about events that were going on. "Stop worrying about white fragility" was a comment I heard more than once. Across the United States, many people of color were leaving multiethnic churches that failed to address real issues pertaining to their communities. One social media warrior even urged people to leave the churches where the pastor did not address specific issues.

Let me be clear: the pulpit is not the place to get on personal soapboxes and push man's agenda; it's all about God's agenda! I deeply believe that the problem with many of us in the body of Christ is that many pastors grossly underestimated how much justice is on the agenda of God. To me, acknowledging injustice is about discipleship and honoring God.

There are some assumptions that pastors must push against if we are ever going to be able to acknowledge any sensitive issues with the congregation.

- *Assumption 1: **We have to choose one issue at the expense of another.*** There have been times when I have addressed the heartache of the senseless killing of a Black man at the hands of a White person and was quickly met with a retort about all the Black people that die at the hands of other Black people. It is similar to the argument from some that if we fight against abortion, then we cannot care about those in poverty and life after the womb. We have the capacity to care for both and we do not have to address everything in order to address some things.
- *Assumption 2: **You have to know all the facts before you can show compassion and empathy.*** I have learned not to give in to the pressure to speak beyond my knowledge of the situation or beyond the clarity that I have gained through prayer. However, when people are hurting because of what is going on in the news, I can call us all to pray. If a life has been lost, I can pray for comfort over people who are mourning; when policies have been issued that affect people in our congregation, I can pray for clarity and peace; when there is a situation that is awaiting a verdict, we can all pray for justice without indicting anyone. I may or may not always change my sermon that week, but we can and should call God's people to prayer, lament, and compassion.
- *Assumption 3: **If we say nothing, the issues disappear.*** A Jamaican-American friend of mine, Roland Fisher, pastors a diverse church in downtown Chicago. He mentioned the problem that comes when we fail to speak on some of these sensitive and racially charged issues: "We leave a vacuum for someone or something else to fill." Choosing to say nothing does not diminish the issues, but it does limit how God is invited into the issue. When we acknowledge and put voice to the issue, we invite God into the problem and lean on him for the solution.

Accountability

Seeking justice starts with honest acknowledgment of what has happened in the past and what is happening now, but that is not the ending point. There must also be accountability. A few years ago, there was a string of events that seemed to come up every other week. It's funny how these racially charged events rarely seemed to take place early in the week but almost always happen on the weekend right after you have prepared your sermon. A string of Black people had died at the hands of police officers, and there were shootings in churches and grocery stores. The question was whether or not people were going to be held accountable for these deaths.

Then there was the 2016 election. Every multiethnic church that I knew of had a difficult time in 2016. It reminded us of how divided we really were. It caused many pastors to come face-to-face with the reality of our wonderful responsibility and opportunity to lead the way in facing difficult racial tension head-on. In his book *With God in the Crucible*, Peter Storey described his conviction as a South African pastor during the time of apartheid: "No ministry in South Africa could have integrity unless it confronted apartheid head-on in the name of Christ."[53] For many believers in South Africa, their conscience and integrity would not allow silence from the church. In each generation, we as pastors must be people of integrity when we face the challenges of our time, and we must call to account the forces that perpetuate injustices.

When we look at this idea of accountability, we are to be a voice of conscience that reminds those in power that we are first and foremost accountable to God. James reminds us of this strong point when addressing the rich and powerful of his day:

> Come now, you rich, weep and howl for your miseries which are coming upon you. Your riches have rotted and your garments have become moth-eaten. Your gold and your silver have rusted; and their rust will be a witness against you and will consume your flesh like fire. It is in the last days that you have stored up your treasure! Behold, the pay of the laborers who mowed your fields, and which has been withheld by you, cries out against you; and the outcry of those who did the harvesting has reached the ears of the Lord of Sabaoth. You have lived luxuriously on the earth and led a life of wanton pleasure; you have fattened your hearts in a day of slaughter. You

---

[53] (Storey, chap. 1)

have condemned and put to death the righteous man; he does not resist you. Therefore be patient, brethren, until the coming of the Lord ..." (James 5:1–7a).

The sins of the rich and powerful were grievous: laborers and harvesters were not being paid what they were worth, and others benefited from their efforts and lived luxurious lives. The righteous had been put to death, and the wicked did not see any resistance against their actions. While it may seem for a while that there is no one to resist your wickedness and exploitation, there is a God to whom you must give account. The Lord is coming! Our understanding of the Lordship of Jesus does not just mean Jesus is the Lord of our personal lives. Even society as a whole will have to give an account to Jesus one day for how people groups, especially those vulnerable to being taken advantage of, were treated. When the poor are taken advantage of, when Black and Brown people are murdered with seemingly no repercussions, when unfair practices give certain people access to resources while ignoring other groups, the church reminds the communities we serve, and sometimes but not always larger platforms, that we will all have to give an account. This does not mean we become passive about seeking accountability now for the sake of waiting till the sweet by and by. It means we seek accountability now because we want to reflect His kingdom on earth as it is in heaven in the here and now.

As leaders in the church, part of seeking justice is being held accountable for how we lead (or fail to lead) in moments of national tension. Over the years, I began to grow in my stance on addressing political and ethnically charged issues. I still do not have an exact formula about figuring out what to address in the news and what not to, and I do not speak to everything that makes the news cycle from the pulpit. At times, when I do address things, I am reminded really quickly of what it feels like to step into a hornet's nest. But a watered-down sense of unity and fear of losing people because I addressed difficult things or took difficult actions will not be the reason for silence, especially when we have an opportunity to bring a Christ-centered perspective in the conversation. Similarly, fear of losing people because I did not go far enough will not be the reason for me to say more or do more than I should say or do at the time, either. I don't want to disappoint my brothers and sisters who expect me to speak on issues that are important, but more importantly, I don't want to disappoint the God who called me into this work of ministry.

For many Black pastors, the problem is not bringing up critical issues, it is how we choose to speak about them. Sometimes courage is demonstrated in a willingness to speak. Other times, courage is our willingness to speak with a tone of forgiveness even if it is mistaken for catering. As Black pastors, we are often tempted to either bypass voicing our need for justice and accountability, thus ignoring real pains and injustices to get to reconciliation, or we stop at justice, not pressing for reconciliation. The gospel neither ignores justice nor stops at justice. Without reconciliation as the goal, we have not preached the gospel. God has given us the ministry of reconciliation. Paul sums up the sentiment that we must have if we are going to speak and lead courageously in this hour: "For am I now seeking the favor of men, or of God? Or am I striving to please men? If I were still trying to please men, I would not be a bond-servant of Christ" (Galatians 1:10).

Advocacy: Restorative Steps in Making Things Right

Our voice as Christian leaders can expand beyond what is heard on a Sunday morning to advocate for more creative solutions to very real problems. Sometimes, there is an opportunity to take practical steps to help make something right that is currently wrong. I use the term "creative solutions" because there are times when situations are complex and require Spirit-empowered leadership to help make situations right for all people, not just a select group of people. Acts 6:1–7 gives us an example of what this looked like in the early church.

In the very first verse, there seems to be a contrasting thought: on the one hand, the number of disciples was increasing, a good thing. But on the other hand, a complaint arose, an indication that something was wrong. You can be in the midst of a move of God and still have issues of disparity to work through. As we continue to read, we see the nature of this complaint: "a complaint arose on the part of the Hellenistic Jews against the native Hebrews, because their widows were being overlooked in the daily serving of food." To understand the context, there are two groups present: the Hellenistic Jews (Greek-speaking Jews who would have grown up outside of Judea and would have more than likely been in town for the Pentecost festival that took place a little earlier) and the native Hebrews (those who grew up in Judea and perhaps would have been seen as the true Hebrews because they knew the language and customs of their forefathers more intimately than those who grew up elsewhere). These two groups, who were changed by the power of Christ, were trying to figure out how to do life together. The problem we see here is that the Hellenistic Jewish widows were being overlooked in the daily serving of food. We do not know if this was done intentionally or simply an administrative oversight. Either way, it was a problem that was systemic in nature; a group of people were not given access to the resources at the same level as another group. Here was the solution in verse 3: "Therefore, brethren, select from among you seven men of good reputation, full of the Spirit and of wisdom, whom we may put in charge of this task." They selected seven men, seemingly those who identified with the marginalized group, to look into the matter and find a solution.

This is how the church leaders responded to this systemic issue: *The leaders listened to the complaint.* They did not rebuke the widows and make the complaining the issue but allowed for the complaints to lead them to the real issue. They leaned into the problem. They brought the community together to address the problem. They worked together to look for people who had the character of God, the Spirit of God, and the wisdom of God to address the issue. This meant that the apostles had to be willing to empower other people to lead. If restitution is going to happen, it will require someone giving up power, privilege, and preference. We do not know the details of what happened, but apparently the situation was addressed because we do not hear about this problem again. As pastors, we may not be called to fix every issue that comes along, but we can create an environment where Spirit-empowered people can lean into creative solutions to make things right.

Here is a modern-day example of another way the church can be involved in the work of acknowledging sin in our nation and advocating to make things right in a way that promotes healing. I was recently made aware of a tragedy that took place in November 1920 in Ocoee, Florida, a town just west of Orlando. A couple of prominent Black men in the city came to cast their vote and were turned away. After coming back with more African Americans, they insisted on voting and were met with more hostility and force. That same day, the sheriff of Ocoee gathered local KKK members to do an ethnic cleansing of the city, leaving more than fifty African Americans dead and many others missing. It was the worst voting massacre that has taken place in the United States since this nation's inception. That same sheriff later became the mayor of the city. Black people lost their lives, their homes, and their right to vote as American citizens all in one fateful election. This tragedy was never acknowledged publicly, and no one was ever held accountable. This became a tragic event that was swept under the rug.

I lived in Orlando for several years but did not learn about this until recently, when a friend of mine, who pastors in that same city, named Keith Tower shared it with me. He told me that the current mayor, a Christian, felt the need to publicly repent of this evil and acknowledge the event and the names of the people who lost their lives senselessly. Several churches, including Keith Tower's church High Point Orlando, worked together with the city to properly bring this up from under the rug and make people aware of this tragic part of our history. Here is an excerpt from Ross Middleton, one of the pastors at High Point Orlando, who was able to see the power of healing of this moment firsthand. He was on the committee to coordinate the weeklong event, which focused on telling the story, honoring the memory, healing the wound, and maintaining hope for tomorrow.

As the week happened, there were countless moments of God showing up in miraculous ways. There are amazing testimonies and stories that have come forth as a result of this. We could truly feel the hand of God leading us along the way.

As the week wrapped up and as we reflected on this week, we realized this was a once in a lifetime type ministry opportunity. Having a public partnership with a city in a pluralistic culture, that is largely hostile to Christianity in the middle of a pandemic is nothing short of a miraculous work of God. It still blows my mind that the church and the city partnered together to bring racial reconciliation. In addition to that, the Governor of Florida, Gov. Ron DeSantis, signed into law that the Ocoee Massacre must be taught in all Florida public schools in the State of Florida history classes moving forward. Teachers will be directed towards using the documentary and materials that were made from this week as one of the source materials to teach to all Florida students moving forward. Only God makes something like that happen in our modern day Babylon. It goes to show how passionate God is about racial reconciliation and righting the wrongs that have happened in our cities all over this nation.

Don't doubt that God would use you to minister in such a profound way to your city. He will, regardless of the cultural narrative about Christianity. He is bigger than any opposition we face. Serve your city well, this didn't happen overnight. It was the favor of God and the result of our church, under the leadership of Pastor Keith and Jennifer Tower, doing an incredible job serving its community well for many, many years before myself and Nikka Warner ever stepped foot in an HRDB meeting. If Keith and Jennifer had not laid that foundation, we would not have experienced the favor we did that night. This opportunity wasn't manufactured overnight, it was a miracle that was years in the making, I just happened to be at the right place at the right time. Make no mistake about this, Jesus did this. We could have never made something like this happen. As Jesus tells us in Matthew 10:16, "… so be wise as serpents and innocent as doves." Look for ways to serve and God will open amazing doors.

Leading in Civil Tension

We as pastors must have the courage to lean into issues of justice and racial tension by seeking acknowledgment, accountability, and advocacy. We cannot violate our conscience for the sake of playing it safe. I remember the words from Pastor Tim Johnson many years ago as I was getting prepared to plant our church in Cincinnati. "If you could lose them you never had them." It is a terrible burden to live with the fear of losing people. Our response as pastors to racially charged events in the news is complex with a lot of opportunities for offending people. Here are a few ways to process these complex situations.

Processing On a Personal level

How am I feeling about things personally? I have to consider how my own heart is doing in light of these things that I am seeing on the news. When George Floyd was murdered for the world to see at the hands of a police officer, I had so many emotions to process and I also felt the pressure, whether internally or externally, to have the right words to say in that moment. I ended up giving myself a day to process through prayer and reading scripture before posting anything, and I was led to Psalm 42. This passage resonated deeply with me because the author went through a range of emotions: "Why are you in despair, o my soul? And why have you become disturbed within me? Hope in God, for I shall yet praise Him, the help of my countenance and my God" (Psalm 42:11). I was reminded that it is possible to love God and still feel despair. I also was reminded that even in despair there is a way back to hope again. This time to personally process was vital for me and for those that I serve as pastor.

Processing on a Pastoral level

I also had to *process pastoring* our people. I want to get the gospel out to as many people as possible, and social media has been a blessing in doing this. But I am also called as a pastor to serve a specific group of people who are wrestling with the same things everyone else is seeing on the news. This means I may need to make personal calls to congregants. I may need to have conversations with some of my White parishioners who are trying to understand the complexity of ethnic tensions and need a healthy space to ask questions and wrestle through questions with grace and truth. Note that there is a difference between people trying to genuinely understand and converse and those who are trying to win an argument. I have seen both, and I only have time for the former.

Processing what I Post

Another layer of processing is *processing our posting* on social media. I am a naturally private person and social media often goes against the very fabric of my wiring. Yet at the same time, this is the world we live in, and people are checking to see what the church has to say about certain issues. My best suggestion here is to be prayerful rather than reactionary in your posting. As my wife will often say, "Pray before posting." Have a diverse team of people who can put eyes on whatever it is that you are posting. There still may be some hard things that need to be posted, but at least do it with your eyes wide open. I also know that as a pastor, whatever I post can be seen as synonymous with what the church is posting.

Processing my Partnerships

When engaging and responding to current events, I also have to *process my partnerships*. The question here is not only what are we supposed to say and do, but who are we supposed to do it with? I have found that key collaborations during difficult times are very important. Recently, after a string of Black deaths at the hands of law enforcement, I partnered with a group of pastors and leaders, and we had a time of prayer, protest, and lament. This was a powerful time where there was repentance, forgiveness, prayer, and the gospel preached. After it was over, the team that coordinated this event discussed what made it successful and the conclusion was that we had relationships that went far beyond a single event. Another reason it was successful was that we were all in alignment in our commitment to the gospel and to speaking truth in love. No one person had to bear that burden alone. The partnerships extended to other organizations doing important work to bring justice and equity to all people.

Processing what I Preach

Finally, we must *process our preaching* when we respond to racially charged incidents. In the book *Practicing the Preaching Life*, David Ward challenges preachers to live lives of courageous justice. He said, "A preacher announcing justice risks painful rejection, lowered church attendance, loss of friendships, removal of ordination, and in some cases the loss of life."[54] We must be sensitive to the Holy Spirit's leading as we speak to our congregations about these issues and have the courage to trust the words that he gives us to speak.

Building Cultural Awareness in the Church

Cultural education starts with relationships. Until we are willing to have multiethnic relationships, we will not understand each other culturally. Each person needs to be committed to growing beyond themselves. We are all joining in together to learn more about ourselves and others at the

---

[54] Ward, 76.

same time. For example, we (Divine Unity Community Church) recently had Restorative Justice healing groups in light of mammoth-sized civil unrest in our culture. This served as a way for people to process and ask questions about how they can understand the pain and plight of people of color. The goal was also to help people become a part of the solution. A white woman, in her mid-sixties and a widow, commented in one of the groups that "in light of all of this, had I not been attending this church, I wouldn't have been able to change as much as I have." Having a Black pastor in the pulpit allowed her to acknowledge a young African American man walking down the street.

Cultural education that is grounded in relationships allows us to close the gap and the skewed perspectives of different people. When the heart is right, it will push people to get the head knowledge to support the conviction. This is the essence of Romans 12–15. The law of love fills in the gaps between us and others. This is a divine partnership that makes way for grace and growth to be present in all parties.

Tips for Black Pastors

Perhaps the challenge you are dealing with is the fear of saying the wrong thing. How do we know what to address and what to not address? Here are a few tips on how to figure out what to address.

1. **The issue affects many people in your congregation.** When President Trump issued an executive order back in 2017 concerning immigration policy, it was not just a conversation piece for many in our congregation; it had very real consequences. To not say anything would have been ignoring the elephant in the room. I have no formula, but many times I know it's on the hearts of our people through conversations and social media. Yes, I said it. Social media can be a source of recognizing issues that need to be addressed.
2. **The issue speaks directly to a gospel issue.** After the murder of Botham Jean, I knew this was the case. Botham was a young Black man who was sitting in his apartment when an officer came into his home and shot him, allegedly by accident. As bad as this

incident was, it was the circumstances surrounding the sentencing that caused a lot of discussion and debate among Christians. At the sentencing of the officer, the brother of the deceased created what I believe was a powerful moment. He was visibly hurt from the entire situation, but in the midst of his pain he extended forgiveness to the officer. He took it a step further and gave her a hug. In comes the debate. Some believers were upset because this seemed to minimize another killing of an innocent Black man by always extending forgiveness. On the other side, people saw this as a beautiful act of love and used Twitter and Facebook to show their appreciation for this brother's actions. The following Sunday, I felt led to preach on "Going Beyond an either/or Gospel." There are many examples like this that we can use as gospel opportunities.

3. **The issue moves you personally.** I realize that personal feelings cannot be the only barometer about what is said and what is not. However, I do believe God has chosen you, including your personality and experiences, to lead your church for a reason. Use discretion and wisdom but know that sometimes the best thing you can do is allow people to see how you really feel about a situation.

4. **The issue is timely.** The late great preacher Rev. Gardner Taylor once said in a lecture, "Our preaching should be both timely and timeless."[55] The timeless aspect should have an eye to the eternal word of God and an eye to the timely and relevant issues of the day. One of the rebuttals that comes up when one current issue is addressed is the question, "What about other issues?" Why do we care about this Black man who was killed when people are killed every day? Why do we care about abortion when there are so many children that are already born and not being taken care of? First, it is possible to care about more than one issue at a time. Second, I believe there are times when God will sovereignly allow some problem in society to come to the attention of a nation or a city at a particular time. Ecclesiastes 3 talks about a time for everything: "There is an appointed time for everything. And there is a time for every event under heaven" (Ecclesiastes 3:1). As I am writing this chapter, our nation is experiencing a time when the racial pain of

---

[55] Taylor, "On Preaching."

our nation cannot be ignored. Is it the results of a liberal agenda making racism an issue in our nation for political gain? Some may believe this to be the case and there will always be people who will use national pain for personal agendas. However, I believe God is forcing us as a nation to deal with the sin of racism and to deal with it now. If we miss God's sovereignty when He allows issues to be brought to the forefront of society, we may well be fighting against God's agenda under the guise of fighting a political agenda.

When you are convinced about an issue affecting people in your congregation and that it is the time to say something, speak with boldness. I encourage you to take the time you need to hear from God's Word *before* speaking. It is better to take a little longer before posting or speaking on something in public than to speak too hastily and miss God's heart on the issue.

Tips for Leaders Supporting Black Pastors

Tips number one, two, and three: Don't leave Black pastors hanging out there to talk about issues alone, especially those dealing with racially charged events. The burden of addressing issues like this often falls on Black people. Speak up and show unity in leadership. If you happen to be White or a different ethnicity, help have the hard conversations with people who are part of your ethnicity. Don't leave all the conversations to your Black pastors. Please and thank you!

Dr. King wrote a letter on April 16, 1963, from a jail in Birmingham, Alabama. In this letter he took time to challenge the church, specifically White pastors who were slow to speak out and stand with him and others fighting against the injustices taking place. The unwillingness of so many brothers and sisters in Christ to address social issues that were morally wrong but legally sanctioned provoked Dr. King to the point that he called them out. He called out the cowardice and false dichotomy that many have created between the gospel and social concerns. Looking back now it makes sense that King would have called fellow Christians to account, but at the time it came off as radical to many. Where are we at risk today of making the same mistake?

Tips for Congregants of Black Pastors

There are some things that you can do if you are struggling to understand some of your pastor's recent decisions or a recent message just did not settle right for whatever reason.

Pray. I know that seems predictable and obvious. But before you send that email of frustration or secretly leave without any announcement, spend time praying for your pastor. Let me let you in on a lesser-known truth: your pastor is probably frustrated about having to address the issue yet again because of a recent shooting. Your pastor was probably not anxiously awaiting the next racially charged incident so they could get back on their horse and spew their thoughts on racism or politics again. Your pastor knows that whatever is said can be potentially divisive to at least one group in the congregation and this may mean losing people. Some in the congregation will be frustrated that they did not say enough. Some will be agitated that they said anything at all.

So pray. Pray for your pastor's ability to hear from God amid all the other voices. Pray for your pastor's personal emotional health. Pray for your pastor's courage. Pray for the people in the congregation who think differently than you do. Pray that Jesus would get exalted even if that means you have to be made uncomfortable for a while.

Listen. James aptly reminds us: "But everyone must be quick to hear, slow to speak and slow to anger" (James 1:19). I believe what we often call listening is actually just waiting for buzzwords that fit into whatever narrative we subscribe to while ignoring the rest of what is said. Few things are as frustrating and divisive as people who refuse to listen or can only listen to people who reinforce what they already believe. If there is something that you need more clarity about, find someone who can help you understand a different point of view. Read a book or listen to a podcast that can explain where people on the "other side" are coming from.

Disagree with graciousness. It's OK to have a different political view or to see issues of race differently than your pastor. He is not infallible and if he claims to be, please leave immediately. But you are not infallible either. It is quite possible that your perspectives on matters are off. If God has called you to be a part of that church, it could be that God is using this moment to change something in your perspective. Give yourself and your pastor room to grow. There is a difference between your pastor preaching heresy and compromise and your pastor having different political and social views than you.

If you find that you cannot take the differences or that your conscience is compromised if you stay, then it is OK to leave and find another church. Do not contribute to bringing division by finding people in the church to slander your pastor or the people in the church that think differently. Do not come to church with a negative attitude because you did not like last week's sermon. And please do not violate your conscience. It is better to just leave. Be honest about why you are leaving. Do not just say "God called us to leave" unless you are sure that it is truly God calling you. Be careful about invoking God's name in your quest to leave a place that you have become dissatisfied with. It may be simply that you prefer another place to worship. Just be honest with yourself and the church that has served you faithfully up to that point. Thankfully, there are other great churches in your town. However, chances are you will find yourself revisiting this issue again unless you choose a church where everyone looks and thinks like you.

Discussion Questions

What are the social issues that need addressing in this world today?
How and where are the best places to address these issues?
What makes you mad in the world today?
What makes you mad in the church today?
What biases did this chapter reveal?
What fears did this chapter reveal?

6

The Question of Currency: Are There Strings Attached?

> At my first defense no one supported me, but all deserted me;
> may it not be counted against them. But the Lord stood with
> me and strengthened me, so that through me the proclamation
> might be fully accomplished, and that all the Gentiles
> might hear and I was rescued out of the lion's mouth.
> (2 Timothy 2:16–17)

The feeling of being alone is something many pastors leading multiethnic churches wrestle with. Someone may take your well-intentioned words the wrong way or people may leave your church because you went too far or not far enough in addressing a recent racially charged incident. But the sense of loneliness is not just an emotional hurdle to overcome, it is often a financial one, as well.

There was an element from my comparative analysis of the challenges leaders of multiethnic churches face that took me by surprise: the role money plays in how pastors lead these churches. For example, how do you address an issue when a big tither may get offended or scared off? What if there is a larger denomination or overseeing body that supports you based on a level of conforming to a normalization that does not fit your vision?

Of course, the answer is just trust God. I don't disagree with that response, but when your employee's family is fed based on people's giving in the church, it is easy to find yourself proceeding with caution when it comes to issues that may rock the boat. Thankfully, this has not been as much of a factor in my personal pastoring experience, but this is not the case for everyone. Many pastors and missionaries have felt the financial impact of trying to navigate in racially and politically charged times. I am grateful for other pastors and leaders who have led the way in thinking through the complexities of this question.

We cannot lead well with the fear of losing people or their financial contributions. Throughout scripture, men of God spoke out in no uncertain terms in a way that made them unpopular with those in positions of power. Even Jesus spoke difficult things to the leaders of His day. When the Pharisees came to Jesus after plotting about how to trap Him in His words, they said, "Teacher, we know that You are truthful and teach the way of God in truth, and defer to no one; for You are not partial to any" (Matthew 22:16). Even the opponents of Jesus recognized that He was unwilling to defer to any man no matter the status or riches that they possessed. We must also take the attitude of Peter and John when they said, "Whether it is right in the sight of God to give heed to you rather than to God, you be the judge, for we cannot stop speaking about what we have seen and heard" (Acts 4:19–20). They were not just threatened with losing finances; they were threatened with losing their freedom and ultimately their lives, but they still spoke with boldness and truth. There may be tithers or significant contributors that drop off because you spoke up on an issue one too many times or sang one too many Fred Hammond songs, but we all must preach and lead with the conviction of the Holy Spirit, not the fear of finances.

Zechariah spoke a message that was challenging to the people of Israel, but he spoke with boldness because it was the Word of God. In Zechariah 11:12 he said: "If it is good in your sight, give me my wages; but if not, never mind!" Even if Zechariah was not going to receive his wages for prophesying God's word, he was going to speak God's word no matter what. I love how Walter Brueggemann once said, "The prophet is never on the payroll of the king."

The following story demonstrates the way ministry finances can be affected when people who support the church financially feel threatened by a pastor's willingness to speak on sensitive issues. This is from an African American missionary who recounted a story with one of his ministry partners:

> It was the summer after another deeply contentious American election cycle, but this one included the unique dynamics of issues of race in a tightly contested race. As an African American missionary, for years I have had a team of people who monthly pray and financially undergird the ministry I serve in. Typically, the summer is a time when my family spends several weeks visiting these partners to personally connect and share stories of what God has done during the year. One of those meetings that summer was eye-opening, though.
>
> I had a ministry partner share with me how they had caught wind I posted something political on my Facebook page and they suggested I be careful not to get too political online. In fact, they went on to say, it had already cost me a ministry partner who got offended on what I had posted. All I could do is laugh in shock! I literally had to go back through to read my post to remember what I posted since I rarely post or repost politically motivated material. What was amazing to me was the only thing I ever posted after the election was that it is a Christian's duty to pray for whoever is elected to serve the people of our land and that I would be praying. The ministry partner I lost simply read into my post and thought I was rubbing in the victory of their opponent! To complicate the situation, this partner was White and the election involved Barack Obama being re-elected to his second term as our first African American president. All of this brought various questions to the surface, namely, are politics and race more important than the gospel's advancement to some of my brothers and sisters in Christ?

I wish this was a rare situation, but this is one of the reasons pastors, especially Black pastors, carry a practical concern about addressing difficult subjects in diverse contexts. He only encouraged prayer for the president, which is very clearly taught in scripture: "First of all, then, I urge that entreaties and prayers, petitions and thanksgivings, be made on behalf of all men, for kings and all who are in authority, so that we may lead a tranquil and quiet life in all godliness and dignity" (1 Timothy 2:1–2). It seems that for some brothers and sisters in Christ, African American pastors and leaders are on a short leash when it comes to their support.

Sometimes the financial concern with leading a multiethnic church is not just for the church, but for the pastors of these churches. I have heard stories of people who spoke too boldly about issues of race and division and lost their jobs as a result. Many people have boards and sending organizations that oversee their pastoral position and have the authority to make changes without the pastor's consent. It is easy to speak about being bold when your family's income is not on the line, but being bold can lead to some difficult choices.

I will note that I've seen firsthand the provision of God when we trust Him in obedience. There have been times when we have made decisions as a church that have been at the risk of offending someone who once supported us. In each situation, God always provided. God has put our church on people's hearts seemingly at random but key times when we needed resources. We have learned to trust in the Lord with all our hearts and lean not to our own understanding. It is our understanding that says play it safe and do not offend potential givers, including parent or larger organizations that support you. It is trusting God with all our hearts that gives us the courage to be moved by our conscience and not by our fear of lack.

Combating the Poverty Mindset and Developing Black Leaders

There is another way that this question of currency comes into play in Black leadership in the church. Growing up in a working middle-class family, I (Chris) did not experience poverty regarding a lack of resources for basic needs. However, I learned later that poverty is not simply about money and property. It is a mindset. The poverty mindset makes one think that there is one pie that supplies slices for everyone, and the more someone else has, the less you will have. It is also the fear of not having enough. I know someone is thinking, "Just trust God." Many Black people have the thought in the back of their minds that White people have more disposable income, and whether that thought is validated by fact or perception, this can condition them toward a poverty mindset with regards to finances. This could be due to generational wealth and opportunity given to Whites versus people of color. Most Blacks are still recovering from years of disparities that have caused educational, psychological, and financial difficulty. The social networks often afforded people exposure and education to financial prowess and wisdom.

For the first three years of our church plant, I was bivocational. I worked forty-plus-hours a week at my job and started a church. The fear of being labeled a prosperity preacher or wanting someone else's money crippled me financially. It took a mindset shift, mentorship, and encouragement from others to start progressing beyond this adopted mindset. This shift did not necessarily increase my personal income or the income of the church, but it helped me make the most of what I had.

My church still in many ways underperforms financially in comparison to other churches in our area. Although my church reaches three times as many people as other churches in the region, our income is nearly equal to those churches'. There are several factors that contribute to this, including the age of the church and general age of the congregation. However, there is another factor that cannot be ignored: ethnic diversity. While our church is multiethnic, we do reach more people of color than other churches in the city. The financial disparity that is sensed in the church at large is reflected in my local context. There seems to be a longer journey for pastors of color to gain the financial trust of the general White population without it being directly connected to a "missional" opportunity or a "savior" opportunity to help an urban church.

On the other hand, I (Brian) have witnessed what happens when churches and organizations are invested in empowering Black leadership and leaders from every ethnicity. Recently, I was with a few pastors outside of a hotel talking past midnight after some meetings. We have not only been part of the same ministry, but we have also been friends for many years. As we began talking about diversity in the church, we began commenting on the number of Black pastors leading multiethnic churches in our family of churches, Every Nation . I have been around the church world long enough to know that this is not normal in most places, but it has become an expectation. Jon Owens, one of the pastors there who leads a great multiethnic church in Indianapolis, made an observation that should have already been obvious to me. What we saw was not accidental; there was intentional financial investment made years ago that contributed to what we are seeing in our movement.

Years ago, there was a resource created by Brett Fuller and Rice Broocks for our ministry called AARM (African American Resource Ministry). It was actually launched first in South Africa (also known as ARM or African Resource Ministries) as a way to remove barriers to Black leaders being released into ministry. At the time, some of our leaders observed that while we had diversity among attendees in our churches in South Africa, there was not diversity seen in the leadership of these churches. This was in large part due to the financial hurdles that were prevalent. In both South Africa and the United States, the A(A)RM scholarship functioned to help raise money to fund African American students to go to conferences and to go into full-time ministry.

I happen to be the recipient of scholarships from AARM. Many leaders that I have talked with have searched for ways to bring diversity to their organizations by hiring out pastors and leaders who are diverse. This is a great start and very necessary. However, an investment must also be made to develop African Americans leaders, not just hire ready-made leaders. This is a long-term commitment, but it can pay dividends by using financial resources to open doors for multiethnic leadership.

Tips for Black Pastors

Brace for the unexpected. This is not really specific to Black pastors and can be applied to all leaders who oversee finances in a church or any organization. But there is a specific application to Black pastors here. How do we brace ourselves for the eventual fallout that may come from the church being too outspoken over certain issues for some people's taste? How do we prepare for larger church organizations that threaten to remove support because we have become too much like the other "radical" Black pastors? Thankfully, I have not seen even a hint of pulling support from our covering denomination, Every Nation, but many pastors have experienced this on a denominational level and on an individual basis with people in their ministry. Here are some suggestions:

1. **Build for financial independence.** Churches should seek sustainability independent of other organizations. Many times, planting a church relies heavily on other institutions. This may include a larger church or a larger denomination providing a significant contribution. Do not get comfortable with being financially dependent on these institutions; let it be a bonus, not the main source of support. This may mean building more slowly or reorganizing the budget. Wean yourself off the support as quickly as possible, not because they demand it but because you desire it.

2. **Be upfront with your vision.** There are a lot of things that get developed along the journey of pastoring: building decisions, new programs, staffing, etc. However, there are certain core convictions that you have from the beginning of either starting a new church or taking over an existing church. The clearer you have thought through those convictions, the better you are able to articulate those convictions. If you have a heart to be multiethnic in your expression of worship, communicate that conviction early and often so people who join your church or give to your ministry know what they are partnering with. If you want to be active in justice issues in your city, communicate it outright. Give people a chance to say whether they want to be a part of your vision.

3. **Be open to multiple streams of income.** Some of my heroes in the gospel are preachers who are bivocational. Many Black pastors work jobs outside of ministry to support the work they are doing with the church and at home. Growing up, my pastors were people who worked nine-to-five jobs and, quite honestly, that was normal. Let me be clear: it is not wrong to look to ministry as your primary source of income. I have lived this way for years. Paul the apostle asked, "If we sowed spiritual things in you, is it too much if we reap material things from you?" (1 Corinthians 9:11). But as ministers of the gospel, we have to be able to do what God has called us to do without the fear of financial repercussions.

Tips for Leaders Supporting Black Pastors

Unfortunately, giving in the church can be a play for power for some, although I suspect this is a small few. It is important that your pastor knows that you are standing with them regardless of the cost of the decision. Do not just support your pastor behind closed doors, but also do it openly. If you lead a department and help oversee a portion of the budget, realize that you may have to find creative ways to do certain things you may want to do.

Tips for Congregants of Black Pastors

You have a responsibility to steward where your money goes, and along with that you have a right to give your resources where you see fit. However, if you find yourself tempted to withdraw your financial contributions because of the latest sermon from your pastor or because the pastor did not say the "right" thing or respond fast enough on social media to the latest situation, consider a few things: Did the ministry or pastor offend you or offend the gospel? Did you talk with the pastor or a church leader to seek clarification on an issue or did you assume a narrative? Do you see your financial contribution as a means to control or a means to contribute? At the end of the day, it is your money, but it is God whom you will answer to for what you did with it. If you stop giving to a particular ministry, be sure it is because God is leading you to do so and not because your political sensitivities were hurt.

Discussion Questions

How have you prepared your church financially for attrition and rainy days?

Have you ever been threatened with the removal of financial contributions?

What adjustments will your ministry need to make if financial contributors leave your church?

What biases did this chapter reveal?

What fears did this chapter reveal?

7

The Question of Courage: Are We Ready to Talk?

> How do I know when I'm on the road to
> reconciliation? When I begin to feel pain.
> —Spencer Perkins

> I have many more things to say to you, but you cannot bear them now
> —John 16:12

Spencer Perkins, the late pastor who not only preached on racial reconciliation but lived it out in a time when it was not popular to do so, wrote something in his book, *More Than Equals: Racial Healing for the Sake of the Gospel*, that has stuck with me for a few years now. He asked, "How do I know when I'm on the road to reconciliation? When I begin to feel pain." Throughout my research, I found that there was one common trait among pastors who successfully led their multiethnic churches through challenging times: they were willing to lean into the hard and painful conversations. The mode of conversation may have looked different, with some hosting panel discussions and others developing materials for small groups to wrestle through together. Whatever the method, the pastors helped facilitate difficult conversations. When the pastor and leadership teams say yes to the conversation, they are also saying yes to the possibility of chaos and even the possibility of pain. The one benefit to avoiding difficult conversations is that there is less room for messiness. However, avoiding the mess is also avoiding the possibility of healthy growth that comes from entering into these conversations.

Early in our church plant, there were a series of racially charged stories in the news about unarmed Black citizens being killed. We decided to have what we called a "courageous conversation" on a Sunday night, a time for people to share their stories, listen, and learn. We made a point to communicate that it was not recorded and opened it primarily to members of our congregation. At the end of the conversation, we took communion together. This event was surely a blessing for our church, right? There were a lot of wins that came from that moment, but there were some difficulties that came to the surface, as well.

I wondered if this Sunday night meeting caused more problems than it solved. People said some things that were misunderstood by others and relationships had to be mended. Feelings were hurt, and although it was never overtly stated, I believe this was the reason some people began to disconnect from our church. I am glad we did it because we learned a lot about our church after that meeting. We realized that just having a good mix of diverse ethnicities in our church was not enough; there was still a lot of work to do.

That was not the last time we had a courageous conversation. We did a series of conversations a couple of years later, and they seemed to go much more smoothly. Of course, there were people who felt nervous about what would come of it, and rightfully so. However, we have learned a lot through our different attempts to lead these conversations. We must be willing to risk the hard conversations to close the gap of perspective. Courageous conversations will demand courage from both the listener and the person being listened to. Kim Okesson, professor of cross communication at Asbury University, remarked on this idea: "Cross-cultural communication is hard work. It requires letting go of the privilege of always being understood and the luxury of acting intuitively."[56]

When you begin the conversations, you must be willing to be in it for the long haul. Courageous conversations are not a short-term solution to

---

[56] Okesson, 2017.

fix any issues of division, bitterness, or bigotry. Your first conversation may bring more issues to the surface instead of fixing them. Wouldn't it be great if we could move on after one good conversation at church and never have to have these conversations again? Unfortunately, it doesn't work that way, so there has to be a willingness to keep coming to the table and having courageous conversations.

As I am writing this, we are in the midst of a global pandemic known as COVID-19. This disease appears to be like the flu but can have catastrophic consequences. The disease has two particularly insidious aspects: symptoms can be mistaken for something less harmful, and people could be asymptomatic carriers and still transmit the disease. This means it is possible to seem fine on the outside, and yet carry something inside of you that could damage yourself and those around you.

I believe this parallels what some of our lives look like as we are dealing with issues of bigotry and hatred. We can look asymptomatic as long as we don't have to lean into the difficult conversations. But that does not mean we aren't carrying something on the inside that could be potentially dangerous if not addressed. I use the word courageous to describe these conversations because they will take courage, especially when unflattering things inside of us are revealed. However, if God reveals it, then God can heal it and even bring redemption. The idea of redemption is restoring something back. The hope in having these courageous conversations is that they will restore relationships and bring healing so that we may reflect kingdom unity to the world.

We have not only opened the door for courageous conversations in our church, but I have seen some great ways other churches are having conversations with their members. At Divine Unity Church, Pastor Chris and his team are conducting healing circles. The name alone tells you the intent of these groups.

Here in Harrisonburg, we recently experienced the difficulty of multiethnic churches during civil unrest. In a time of unrest, many people are searching for their place, a place where they could deal with their guilt, and comfort in a modern-day race war of sorts. For the first time in our modern history, people in all fifty states were protesting injustice, police brutality, and systemic racism. For many Black people, it was a harsh reminder that the color of Black skin is criminalized, and that the stench left by slavery– racism, bigotry, and hatred is still alive. This harsh reality is a reminder of the bloody and demonic history of race in the United States. The Black response ranges from people being awakened to this reality with anger, bitterness, and pain to others who are almost numb to it because they have seen it all their lives and are tired.

The White response in my sector has been interesting. Of course, social media, the Wikipedia of people's souls, has revealed quite a bit. As Confederate statues were being taken down in Virginia, one longtime White friend, who I would even say was once a mentor, made a comment that was difficult to digest. He said in a social media post: "If being sad to see a statue of Stonewall Jackson [fall] makes me a racist, then I will always be a racist who loves black people." This comment made me cringe. In the height of this struggle, some White people have taken to defending their nationalism under the cover of Christianity. Whether this conversation takes the direction of White fragility, White guilt, or White privilege, people are trying to figure out if they are racist or not. But the base of my question to White people is not: "Are you racist?" My heart is this: "Are you willing to understand my perspective? Are you willing to sympathize with the generational pain that this country has afforded Black people? Are you willing to be an advocate for justice and reconciliation?"

We cannot dismiss the reality of the struggle that the United States is in. Justice is not an American thing, or a people of color thing, or a minority versus majority thing; justice is a God thing. We, as humans, have hijacked the term justice to fit whatever narrative we desire rather than allowing the justice of God to shape our perspective of other humans. I was recently reading through Amos, and during the first two chapters, God was pronouncing judgment on different nations. What was the primary crime they were being punished for? Crimes against humanity. People mistreated God's creation, and God's command in the book of Amos to fix this was Amos 5:24: "But let justice flow like water, and righteousness, like an unfailing stream." The book of Micah says something very similar: "The LORD God has told us what is right and what he demands: 'See that justice is done, let mercy be your first concern, and humbly obey your God'" (Micah 6:8).

Having courageous conversations that uproot deep-seated trauma is never easy. Especially because we live in a broken world and are surrounded by systems that support continued oppression and supremacy. But we are commanded by God to pursue justice with mercy and walk humbly before God. This will yield a pattern of repentance and deeper relationships. But you cannot correct nor connect where you have not confronted.

It wasn't until the 2020 trifecta of the murders of George Floyd, Ahmad Aubrey, and Breonna Taylor that these conversations were thrust into the forefront of many churches. Leaders scrambled to get their best racial reconciliation and justice messages prepared and presented to churches. Others ignored it and went on "preaching the Bible." Other leaders had a sigh of relief that represented: "finally, everyone sees." My concern with the first two responses of leaders is that they either ignored it before, or do not believe it now. Some people legitimately did not know that racism was still so alive. Whether that's due to privilege or ignorance, 2020 served as a rude awakening. Now people were ready to have some real conversations. But there was another problem. People discovered that even in a multicultural church, they were living segregated lives.

Whether you are a Black pastor, or pastor of any ethnic background, leadership in the church will require courage. We are not telling you anything that you do not know, especially if you are presently engaged in leading a multiethnic church. However, one of the clearest ways this courage can be exercised is in leading healthy conversations in your church. You may find that there is much more work to be done than you anticipated, but you also may find that God's grace in your congregation to reflect His multiethnic kingdom is greater than you anticipated as well.

Tips for Black Pastors

The key here is for Black pastors to lean into the conversation about issues of race. Bring other voices into these conversations when it's appropriate. Assume that people in your congregation need to grow in this area, and don't wait until a national tragedy happens to prompt these conversations. I realized that before we could have these conversations with the rest of the church and community, we needed to have them with each other as a church staff. We have a very diverse staff, and from time to time we have difficult conversations about what we believe and experience concerning race and cultural differences. They are not always easy, but they always lead to growth in one way or another.

Set the conversation in scripture. The Bible has so much to say about our intrinsic value as people created in the image of God. Conversations surrounding topics of racism and justice should be seen as part of our growth as followers of Jesus, not simply a sidebar issue. I believe the best way to grow in our ability to lead these conversations with other believers is to grow in our ability to exposit God's Word.

Utilize helpful resources. There are great tools available that are grounded in scripture and also capture the reality of racism today. Here are a few that have been beneficial to me: *Multiethnic Conversations Primer* by Oneya Okuwobi and Mark DeYmaz; *Race, Injustice, and Discipleship* by Every Nation, *Dreaming in Black and White* by Bishop Brett Fuller, and *Undivided* by Chuck Mingo. I have seen conversations modeled from the pulpit, as well. Bishop Brett Fuller has had several conversations with police officers in his city to help open dialogue about policing practices that often affect one demographic differently than others. There have been many conversations between pastors of different ethnicities where tough questions were asked, and even tougher answers were given.

One such example was with two people I know and love: Pastors Tim and Le'Chelle Johnson (black) and Pastors Andy and Amy King (White). Although the conversation was public, it opened the door for more conversations among congregants to take place on a more personal level. The key to that discussion was the relationship and history between the pastors. Which is why I say again, if we want a multiethnic church, we need a multiethnic life. There are many more examples and resources out there. Find one that fits your congregational context.

Tips for Leaders Supporting Black Pastors

Lean into the conversations with the Black pastors you support. Model courage by admitting ignorance when necessary, speaking truth even when it hurts, and display a willingness to keep coming back to the table for conversation. Do the work of educating yourself on issues surrounding race and history. Reading this book is a good start. Read and listen to others, as well.

Tips for Congregants of Black Pastors

Don't run from the conversations, and don't run from your church when the conversations get difficult. These conversations may happen in a formal way but are more likely to occur in an informal way. The easier thing will be to throw missiles at your proverbial straw men; however, a lot of growth can happen when conversations take place. We must be "quick to listen, slow to speak, and slow to become angry" (James 1:19). But do not remain silent about things that need to be communicated, especially if you have been hurt or offended by someone else. Unfortunately, some problems do not self-correct, and part of us growing up as the body of Christ is speaking truth to one another. Ephesians 4:15–16 says: "… But speaking the truth in love, we are to grow up in all aspects into Him who is the head, even Christ, from whom the whole body, being fitted and held together by what every joint supplies, according to the proper working of each individual part, causes the growth of the body for the building up of itself in love."

Discussion Questions

Has your church created any healthy spaces for courageous conversations?
What tools would best fit your context to help with conversations?
What risks do you have in creating dialogue around issues of race?
What barriers do people in your church have to overcome to be part of these conversations?
What biases did this chapter reveal?
What fears did this chapter reveal?

8

The Question of Conviction: Is It Worth the Headache?

―――― ∞ ――――

Hold on don't you ever let go.
—Fred Hammond, "A Song of Strength"

There are easier ways to pastor than trying to do it as a multiethnic church, and there are easier ways to have multiethnic churches than empowering Black pastors to lead them. Pastoring and leading are already hard enough. The real question becomes, "*Why do it?*" I have heard the sentiment that the multiethnic church experiment did not work in America. Racism still exists in the Church, and it often feels as if we are just as divided as ever. Why push forward with fighting for multiethnic churches? At the end of the day, the reason I pastor a multiethnic church and do it willingly as a Black pastor is because this is what God desires for me to do. I am convinced that in spite of the headaches that come along with leading this way, it is still worth it. A good place to start answering the "why" question is to start with theology.

The theology of diversity is seen in the very Trinitarian nature of God. The doctrine of the Trinity states there is one God who eternally exists in three persons: Father, Son, and Holy Spirit. The key here is that we are talking about one God, not polytheism. However, in the Godhead there is diversity. This is seen in God's roles and functions. We see the Father primarily in the role of Creator, the Son in the role of Redeemer, and the Holy Spirit in the role of Sanctifier. The Father sent the Son, and the Father and Son sent the Holy Spirit. The Holy Spirit sends the church and brings attention to the work of Christ in the heart of the believer, and the Father and Son live in the hearts of believers through the Holy Spirit.

The body of Christ is to reflect God's *imago dei* in the earth. With all these distinct roles, Jesus could also say that He and the Father are one (John 10:30). There is unity in God's diversity. Stephen Seamands, professor and author, captures this reality by stating, "Our diversity in unity mirrors the diversity in unity of the Trinity. Equality, intimacy, submission and deference ought to characterize relationships in the Christian community as well" (Seamands, chap. 2). We reflect the image of God when we show people from different backgrounds and ages what it looks like to follow Christ together in community by learning to defer and submit to one another. Paul said in Ephesians 3:10 that the "manifold wisdom of God might now be made known through the church to the rulers and authorities in the heavenly places." The word used for manifold means marked by diversity or variety. Our diversity reflects the diversity of God Himself.

While the doctrine of the Trinity calls for the Church to reflect God's diversity, the doctrine of soteriology can be reflected in the way the Church pursues diversity. Soteriology is the doctrine of salvation in Jesus Christ. Jesus, who is the Word that became flesh, and came and lived among the people He created. Although He lived a sinless life (Hebrews 4:15), He suffered at the hands of sinful men. Through this sacrificial act of laying His life down for us on the cross, Jesus did for us that which we were unable to do for ourselves: obtain salvation. As Paul states in 1 Corinthians 15:3: "Christ died for our sins."

What makes this act so powerful is not just what Jesus did, but whom He did it for. Even in His final agonizing moments on the cross, Jesus cried, "Father forgive them for they do not know what they are doing" (Luke 23:34). Jesus was not holding their actions against them, even though they deserved punishment. Romans 5:8 tells us that "God demonstrates His own love towards us, in that while we were yet sinners, Christ died for us." When Peter preached about Jesus to the crowd gathered on Pentecost, he reminded them that the Savior of the world was "this Jesus whom you crucified" (Acts 2:36). Because all of us have sinned, we can identify with being transgressors against the only one who is sinless.

How does this relate to the topic at hand? In the gospel, we see it is the offended that pursued the offender. The one who was abused and killed was also the one who extended the opportunity for reconciliation. When we look at the history of the United States, Black people have clearly experienced oppression at the hands of White oppressors. For me, it's not only the experiences dating back to my great forefathers; I know this from family members who are alive right now at the time of this writing. While this may seem like a generalization and does not mean that all Whites are guilty of oppressing all Blacks, we cannot ignore the narrative of racial oppression against Blacks in the United States. If the multiethnic movement is going to reflect the gospel of reconciliation in the United States, groups that have historically been oppressed will have to be a part of extending a hand to those who in some way identify with the oppressors. It is for this reason of reflecting the gospel that Black pastors must lead congregations of people from all nations. It is worth the headaches and challenges that come in order to reflect the beauty of the gospel.

This question of conviction is not just for Black pastors. The burden of this message has often fallen on Black pastors without the support of our brothers and sisters of other ethnicities. If you are non-Black but you desire to empower more Black leaders, if you are on a staff with a Black pastor or desire to bring one on staff, if you are in seminary and thinking of one day seeing a diverse church built, you are going to have to be willing to lean in even when it hurts. It must be more than a good idea; it must be something that you are committed to follow through on.

I'm Still a Black Pastor

It seems fitting to include a section that deals with a real dilemma that can be hard to articulate, but is often palpable for Black pastors leading multiethnic churches: where do we fit in? Being a Black pastor and having a Black congregation seem to go hand in hand. When I am talking with people who know my profession but do not know my congregation, they often assume that I lead a Black church. In reality, I lead a church with around 50% Black people in it, but there are a significant number of people of other ethnicities, as well. In settings with Black clergy, there is often a feeling that we are not quite as included as we might have been if we were leading all Black churches. This may be due to reality or our own inaccurate metaperceptions. But we are not always quite at home in the White evangelical space, either. In both scenarios, the feelings of not quite fitting in could be a combination of internal wrestling and external complexities.

In some ways, this question of fitting in brings together the previous six questions we have discussed in this book. When we talk about credibility, in many ways it goes in two directions. For the White congregants and White clergy, the question is whether or not we are credible enough to lead them; for many Black clergy, the question is whether I am credible enough to represent the Black voice and the Black agenda. Are we still connected to issues of Black concern, or have we simply become ventriloquists who only echo the concerns and viewpoints of some other White leader behind the curtains? Do we think we have become too good for the Black church and believe that our ministry is only validated when White people sign off on it?

In the question of culture, I need to be mindful of how congregants across ethnic lines connect with the culture of the church (i.e., preaching, music, dress code, and other programs within the church). The church culture that I grew up in is much different than the church culture at the church I now lead. I was raised in the Black church, but the majority of my development as a minister vocationally was shaped in a much more diverse space. Both of those realities are part of my story, and both of these realities influence the church I pastor in Cincinnati. At the same time, we are part of the lineage of Black preaching that has helped to build the United States. I have heard stories from my father and uncles about my great-great-grandfather who started and pastored a lean-to church as a former slave. Growing up, my parents were both highly involved in the Church of God in Christ, a predominantly African American denomination, and I witnessed their commitment to the church's work. I did not lose that heritage when I planted a multiethnic church. Black preachers in multiethnic churches identify with preachers who have gone before us such as John Jasper, Gardner Taylor, C.T Vivian, G.E. Patterson, T.D. Jakes, and countless others. But sometimes, for Black pastors leading multiethnic churches, there can be feelings of disconnect from this tradition. It is in these moments that we ask ourselves if it is worth it.

To some degree, I understand the potential hesitation that many of my fellow Black clergy and congregants feel when they see Black pastors in multiethnic spaces. Black people have had to deal with White institutions taking the best and brightest from the Black community, leaving the Black community with less than they had before. When I first went to college on a football scholarship to Vanderbilt University, a debate that still lingers today surfaced about whether or not top Black athletes should go to historically Black institutions instead of predominantly White institutions.

I was raised in the Black church and introduced to Jesus in the Black church. It was the pastors and deacons there, my father included, who modeled to me a life of faith and faithfulness. I am especially grateful for Bishop Steve Coleman of Williams Temple in Portland, Maine, and Bishop Herman Crocket of Faith and Hope Temple in Petersburg, Virginia. I'm also grateful for the church mothers who showed me how to pray and tarry before the Lord. My choir director taught me how to harmonize, and the community taught me how to worship. It was in the Black church that I learned Black history and felt at home when I lived in a world that did not always validate me. It was the Black church that taught me how to sit in church and not fall asleep or make jokes when the pastor is preaching. It was the Black church that celebrated me going to college and getting a scholarship. When I grew up, went to college, and got ministered to by a predominately White ministry (at least at the time; it later became more ethnically diverse), it did not negate all that I learned before that time. I've grown to deeply appreciate all the different voices that have helped to shape me from my childhood to adulthood. Anyone who has studied the Church in scripture knows there is no Black church and White church, just the church. Yet there are faith communities in this nation that have been formed in response to a racialized environment. I long for the day when the term multiethnic church is a redundant term. However, I am still a Black pastor, and I still love the Church. That will never change, no matter how ethnically diverse my church grows to be.

I was reached on the college campus at a time in my life when I was spiritually vulnerable. I am grateful that God sent a Latino minister and a White minister to meet me where I was on the campus. God used this ministry to help me grow as a disciple of Jesus and help others grow in their faith, as well. But I would not have been as ready or open to respond on the campus if I did not have the years of ministry and love that came from my experience growing up in a predominantly Black church environment.

In many ways, being a Black pastor of a multiethnic church is like being in an interracial marriage. For some, it is really celebrated; for others, it is looked down upon. One of the unspoken perspectives is that Black people that are in interracial marriages are looked at as less Black. So many times, the multiethnic church is looked at as a White church with Black people in it. There is a looming fear or thought that as a Black pastor of the multiethnic church, I will lose my "Black card," which is a colloquialism to say I am not culturally authentic or relevant.

My (Chris) exposure to diverse ecclesial and ministry settings allowed truth to challenge cultural norms and expanded my ability to think beyond just my experience or exposure. Things that I thought were true were really cultural. Exposure, education, and empowerment are three things that help people grow. Exposure is what you have seen or been exposed to, and education is what you are taught intentionally and unintentionally. Because I was taught in a traditional Black church setting, a lot of my systematic theology was shaped in this particular environment. The practice of reading the Bible came from a Black, charismatic theological setting. There was appropriate emphasis on hope, freedom, and perseverance. People who were non-academically trained to study the Bible helped keep a level of vibrancy that depended on the Spirit.

In seminary and academic settings, sometimes that vibrancy of the Spirit is lost behind the idolatry of accuracy. It's almost like you go from a humble place of asking, "God, what are you saying?" to an academically-led scientific interpretation. Combining the scientific interpretation and Holy Spirit inspiration of scriptures made way for a clearer vision. It was like going from color TV to HD, then going from HD to 4k. It is the same picture, but you can see it more clearly.

This is also the way that Derwin Gray described the multiethnic church in his book *HD Leader*. This vibrancy and conviction helped me wrestle with scripture in a unique way. Having been raised Baptist, there was a certain doctrine ingrained in the actual church service. But because the word doctrine was not used, I did not know that I knew doctrine. I began to learn things that they did not teach me as I studied in the charismatic setting. As I continued to learn, I was brought back to my roots in the Baptist church. Attending seminary in a Mennonite setting taught me how to do inductive Bible studies and engage in a contemplative spirituality, which helped me see God and scripture in a different way. It expanded my consciousness of scripture and what living theology is. Because I was in these different settings, I was able to learn scripture, church, and ministry from people of different ethnic backgrounds, cultural backgrounds, educational experiences, and social economic classes. This ultimately led to an approach to ministry that begged for diversity and did not void truth.

Tips for Black Pastors

Did God call you to do this or was it a good idea? This is a question that you need to ask yourself before starting a multiethnic church or attempting to transition a church to become ethnically diverse. It's a question we must revisit often. Jeremiah's commissioning in Jeremiah 1 is a scripture that is often referenced to encourage people in their calling: "Before I formed you in the womb I knew you, and before you were born I consecrated you; I have appointed you a prophet to the nations" (Jeremiah 1:5). There is excitement in knowing God has called you, but excitement was not the only emotion Jeremiah felt; he was being thrown into a difficult ministry assignment. Jeremiah's response was somewhat understandable, especially knowing what he was being told to do: "Then I said, Alas, Lord God! Behold, I do not know how to speak, because I am a youth" (Jeremiah 1:6). God responded to Jeremiah with words that resonate with me and anyone attempting to lead a multiethnic church today.

Throughout Jeremiah 1, God tells Jeremiah what not to do: "Do not say, I am a youth, because everywhere I send you, you shall go, and all that I command you, you shall speak" (Jeremiah 1:7). It is easy to find yourself questioning whether or not you are the one for the job. Jeremiah's concern was his youth. Your concern may be whether or not you have enough seminary training, or whether or not you are articulate enough, or any other concern under the sun. God instructs Jeremiah, and us, not to look at our lack of qualifications. Remember, God is the one who appointed Jeremiah and God is the one who has appointed you. Our job is not to question, but to obey. We shall go where God sends us, even if that means going to a group of people who make you uncomfortable, and we are to say what God wants us to say, even if it means saying something that makes other people uncomfortable.

There is another "do not" in verse 8: "Do not be afraid of them, for I am with you to deliver you, declares the Lord" (Jeremiah 1:8). Jeremiah not only had to face his sense of inadequacy; he had to deal with his sense of fear. His fear was not unwarranted because he was sent with a challenging message to a stiff-necked people. Later in Jeremiah, he faces persecution. He is ridiculed, beaten, and unjustly thrown in prison for being obedient to God. Just because God called us does not mean we are exempt from the challenges that are going to come. There may be times when you will be misunderstood and seen as selling out the gospel for the Black agenda, and other times you will be seen as selling out your Black brothers and sisters for the sake of cheap reconciliation. But here is what the Lord said to Jeremiah: "Do not be afraid of them, for *I am with you* to deliver you, declares the Lord (Jeremiah 1:8, emphasis mine).

The third "do not" is found later in Jeremiah's opening chapter: "Do not be dismayed before them, or I will dismay you before them" (Jeremiah 1:17). The term here for dismayed means to be shattered or disheartened. There have been some points throughout my pastorate in Cincinnati that have been disheartening. I remember the 2016 election. It was a divisive time in our nation, and many people were split right down racial lines. People did not have any problems letting others know what they felt about current issues on social media, and it led to quite a bit of tension amongst congregants. People did not want to worship with others who voted differently from them or those who looked different from them. There were Facebook wars among believers, and in the midst of it, people got mad at me for either saying too much or not saying enough. In many ways it felt disheartening. I had to remind myself that these are not my people, but God's people, and this church was not my good idea, it was God's idea.

Tips for Leaders Supporting Black Pastors

The same question that was asked for Black pastors is relevant for any leader supporting Black pastors leading multiethnic churches: Is this a conviction or a good idea? Are you committed to promoting

Black leadership in diverse settings? It is easy to love the idea of being multiethnic, but it is an entirely different story when that same diversity seems to cause more headaches. Do you believe this is worth it? Answer this question intentionally and overtly; sometimes you may have to answer this question multiple times, but answer the question. When the church and the community see a team of leaders, and not just a single leader, standing together to break down walls of division, it becomes a powerful statement to the world.

Tips for Congregants of Black Pastors

Did God call you to be at the church you are at in this season? Paul reminds us in 1 Corinthians 12:18 that "God has placed the members, each of them, in the body, just as He desired." There are times when God calls you to move on to another church. But if God has called you to stay, do not leave simply because your Black pastor is suddenly making you uncomfortable. If your pastor is doing their job, then you will feel uncomfortable at times. Be sensitive and obedient to God's voice, not just your temporary emotions or feelings of discomfort.

Discussion Questions:

What biblical convictions do you have about building and leading an ethnically diverse church?

Have you ever had to wrestle with discouragement when it comes to diversity in the church?

Have you felt like you were in this fight alone?

What biases did this chapter reveal?

What fears did this chapter reveal?

9

Question of Collaboration: Can We Mutually Submit?

> And be subject to one another in the fear of Christ.
> —Ephesians 5:21

Few words have been met with greater suspicion in the body of Christ as the word "submit." We cannot honestly read the Bible and get away from this word. In the New Testament alone we see wives being directed to submit to husbands, children submitting to parents, and slaves being told to submit to masters. At times the idea of submission has been used as a tool to ensure that those in power stay in power and those in subservient roles stay in their place. When pastors step beyond the walls of their church to work with other leaders in the city, the question of who is in charge is often a ubiquitous question that hinders collaboration. Yet when we read scripture, we learn that submission is not a one-way street. Ephesians 5:21 tells us to "subject ourselves to one another in the fear of Christ." There is a beauty in mutual submission because it is there that true collaboration in the body of Christ can take place, and it is there that we see God's people from all ethnicities walking in their God-given leadership.

Francis Chan once said: "The gospel message is incomplete without the picture of the unified church. There is no plan B."[57] The Church is the one place that is supposed to model unity, collaboration, and mutual respect. However, the church has in many ways been an example and contributor to segregation and division. The body of Christ is empowered and designed for collaboration beyond class, culture, and color. As explored earlier, Ephesians 4:1–6 presents a picture of the church that models oneness and unity. The church is one body with many members that is meant to model and promote a collaboration that testifies to the power and work of the Holy Spirit. Shared responsibility, mutual respect, and exponential progress are the essence of collaboration. Collaboration can be both a challenge and dream for some. Typically, people or organizations collaborate because they see value in one another that will create a bigger and brighter future. Collaboration requires a few things: Vision, humility, competence, and conviction.

Vision. This idea of collaboration is at the core of the church at large. When we read Romans 12:1–4, we see that collaboration is the result of true transformation:

> 1. Therefore, brothers and sisters, in view of the mercies of God, I urge you to present your bodies as a living sacrifice, holy and pleasing to God; this is your true worship. 2. Do not be conformed to this age, but be transformed by the renewing of your mind, so that you may discern what is the good, pleasing, and perfect will of God. 3. For by the grace given to me, I tell everyone among you not to think of himself more highly than he should think. Instead, think sensibly, as God has distributed a measure of faith to each one. 4. Now as we have many parts in one body, and all the parts do not have the same function.

The unique blend of people and levels of spirituality presented multiple challenges for the Roman church. There were slaves and freed people, women and men, Jews and Gentiles—everyone was there by God's grace. Our collective and continued need for God's grace is an equalizer. In order

---

[57] Francis Chan, *Until Unity*, 96.

for them to do what God required of them, there were a few things that they had to realize. First, the renewing of their minds transforms them into the image of Christ. Paul's ultimate desire was for them to embody the likeness of Christ. This transformation that they were to undergo was a step toward operating as a collective unified body. Second, renewing their minds separated the believers from the outside pressures of the world. This is a call to distinctiveness and continual transformation. Verse 3 introduces Paul's ethical appeal that the believers think right (verse 3), live unified as the body of Christ (verses 4–8), and love one another (verses 9–15 and chapter 13).

Humility. As we move on to Romans 12:3, Paul says: "Do not think of yourself more highly than you ought, but rather think of yourself with sober judgment." The transformation of the mind allows us to now live unified as one body. Humility is not about dismissing culture, ethnicity, or gender. Humility helps all of those distinctions be properly submitted to the lordship of Christ, and then used to represent the oneness that results through the reconciliation of the Cross.

Humility is a pathway to progressing in Christ, and within community, humility is often connected with the practice of submission. That word submission does not mean simply to agree, it actually takes on the much greater weight of surrender. It was once said that a leader does not know who is truly submitted to their leadership until the leader makes a decision that the follower does not agree with. How the person responds to the disagreement shows whether they are submitted or not.

By no means would I say anyone should submit to something that is unbiblical or harmful. However, there are preferences that must be laid aside for collaboration to happen. The set of disruptions and challenges in 2020 and 2021 truly revealed whether people were submitted to leadership or not. Many Whites left leaders who supported organizations that supported a fight against injustice. Other White congregants angrily detested their pastors for grieving, lamenting, and repenting of the sin of racism. In a peculiar way, tension around racism in this current form has caused a great deal of havoc among many White Christians. The combination of pandemic, civil unrest, and political polarization has made the journey of collaboration a trying road. It has caused people to wrestle with how much social justice is too much for White people and their Christianity. The world would love for the church to be divided, so as leaders we must model a humble approach that reflects the gospel and not a political agenda or a specific culture. Humility is an essential part of unity and an act of love. People can disagree, but without humility, a disagreement on a cultural matter becomes a divide in spiritual places.

Throughout the turmoil of 2020 and 2021 and the effects of those years, I witnessed a loss of humility and love that caused great divides among churches. At a time when the church should have had a greater unified front, we were entangled. Instead of operating as citizens of the kingdom and exiles in the world, many functioned more like citizens of the United States and exiles of heaven. As I read the closing exhortations of humility, love, and unity in Paul's letter to the Romans, it was as if people forsook these principles of Christianity and confused rights with righteousness. Jesus clearly says that we will be known as His disciples by the way we love one another. While there are several issues represented and neglected in political parties, I am reminded that there isn't a political party nor governmental structure that can replace the church's role in society to model love, harmony, justice, and collaboration. Our hope is not in a vote; it is in Christ alone. Anything else or anyone else that is being glorified as a savior is a stumbling block. Romans 12–15 teaches us how to engage with a fallen world without falling. As believers, we have been given a ministry of reconciliation that is a result of transformation through Christ, and that leads to collaboration for Christ.

I want to draw our attention back to Romans 12, specifically Romans 12:9–18. Can you slowly read this with me:

> 9. Let love be without hypocrisy. Detest evil; cling to what is good. 10. Love one another deeply as brothers and sisters. Take the lead in honoring one another. 11. Do not lack diligence in zeal; be fervent in the Spirit; serve the Lord. 12. Rejoice in hope; be patient in affliction; be persistent in prayer. 13. Share with the saints in their needs; pursue hospitality. 14. Bless those who persecute you; bless and do not curse. 15. Rejoice with those who rejoice; weep with those who weep. 16. Live in harmony with one another. Do not be proud; instead, associate with

the humble. Do not be wise in your own estimation. 17. Do not repay anyone evil for evil. Give careful thought to do what is honorable in everyone's eyes. 18. If possible, as far as it depends on you, live at peace with everyone.

It is my hope that there will be a return to the scriptures in all spheres of leadership and reconciliation. Our highest level of humility must be before the Lord, and then we will continually be transformed. Humility is the greatest invitation to God's activity in and through our lives. Christ desires to express Himself through us to this world.

Competence. Cultural competence has become a chief skill in the twenty-first century among organizations and churches. With society rapidly changing and awareness of disparities more evident, cultural competence allows people to cross lines of division with greater compassion and respect. Research on this topic has yielded this definition and description:[58]

> Cultural competence is the ability of a person to effectively interact, work, and develop meaningful relationships with people of various cultural backgrounds. Cultural background can include the beliefs, customs, and behaviors of people from various groups. Gaining cultural competence is a lifelong process of increasing self-awareness, developing social skills and behaviors around diversity, and gaining the ability to advocate for others. It goes beyond tolerance, which implies that one is simply willing to overlook differences. Instead, it includes recognizing and respecting diversity through our words and actions in all contexts.

This sociological perspective encourages people to recognize, advocate, and be intentional with overcoming cultural barriers. The apostle Paul dedicated the latter part of the book of Romans to cultural competence. He even pointed out how our cultural competence can lead to healthy spiritual relationships with brothers and sisters from other cultural backgrounds.

---

[58] Index, Youth & Families, Families, February 2016

What Paul suggested were practical steps of loving our neighbor and not causing them to sin, or unnecessarily offending them. Let us take a moment to read Romans 14:13–23 CSB:

> 13. Therefore, let us no longer judge one another. Instead decide never to put a stumbling block or pitfall in the way of your brother or sister. 14. I know and am persuaded in the Lord Jesus that nothing is unclean in itself. Still, to someone who considers a thing to be unclean, to that one it is unclean. 15. For if your brother or sister is hurt by what you eat, you are no longer walking according to love. Do not destroy, by what you eat, someone for whom Christ died. 16. Therefore, do not let your good be slandered, 17. for the kingdom of God is not eating and drinking, but righteousness, peace, and joy in the Holy Spirit. 18. Whoever serves Christ in this way is acceptable to God and receives human approval. 19. So then, let us pursue what promotes peace and what builds up one another. 20. Do not tear down God's work because of food. Everything is clean, but it is wrong to make someone fall by what he eats. 21. It is a good thing not to eat meat, or drink wine, or do anything that makes your brother or sister stumble. 22 Whatever you believe about these things, keep between yourself and God. Blessed is the one who does not condemn himself by what he approves. 23. But whoever doubts stands condemned if he eats, because his eating is not from faith, and everything that is not from faith is sin.

Paul knew that the gospel was meant to spur one another on, not hold one another back. This passage is much more than "eating and drinking, but righteousness, peace, and joy in the Holy Spirit." Paul addresses religious restrictions that began to erode newfound relationships through the gospel. The cultural competence led to greater levels of compassion, and ultimately understanding the true freedom that was awarded us through the gospel. We are not made righteous through following rules, but we testify of our righteousness through relationships. The ultimate measure of the Christian is found in their love for God and then their neighbor. Unfortunately, much of our church culture has been eroded by judgment rather than collaboration. We have been pointed more toward what divides rather than what and who has saved us. We have been taught to divide where we disagree, rather than strive for unity. Instead of doing the difficult work of learning and valuing others, we segregate ourselves from those different from ourselves. Paul exhorts the people to do what promotes the peace of the gospel. So I suggest that the Holy Spirit leads us to greater levels of cultural competence because we are striving toward likeness in Christ, rather than asking people to be like us.

Conviction serves as a holy anchor for a high call: to live, love, and lead like Christ. In John 16:8, we see a pithy, yet full statement of the work of the Holy Spirit. John 16:8 in the New Living Translation says: "And when He comes, He will convict the world of its sin, and of God's righteousness, and of the coming judgment." Conviction is a work of the Spirit. And the conviction of the Holy Spirit is a trifecta for the human soul. This conviction helps us understand what offends God (*convicts the world of sin*). This conviction helps us understand how to please God (*convicts the world of righteousness*). This conviction reminds me that Jesus will return, and all things will be judged by Him, including the ruler of this world. From the pulpit commentary, I understand that *conviction = holy convincing* that God's way is right.

The world under the depressing and distracting influence of its own principles, as well as its passions, has misconceived the whole nature of "sin," the entire mystery of "righteousness," the certainty of retribution, a den the things and principles on which consign "judgment" must fall. The advocate, the divine, indwelling Spirit of the truth, whom Christ will send into His disciples as compensation for His own absence, will through them do this strange and tremendous work. Our Lord does not here promise the conversion of mankind, but such a conviction that the blessed consequences may follow.

Striving for a divine vision in a secularized society takes holy convincing from heaven. To lead a multiethnic church in the midst of divisive culture, leaders need an anchor that is not found in this world nor the people of it. To collaborate in the realm of church leadership and multiethnic ministry is not a rescue mission, it is a reconciliation mission. Conviction for this work is being readied with a biblical vision of the multiethnic church and biblical wisdom that helps churches and cities get a glimpse of heaven.

As we consider the implications of collaboration, it goes even further than our ability to be at peace with one another; it opens the door for us to be on a mission with one another. How can we pull resources together for kingdom impact in the body of Christ including our money, our collective intellect, and manpower? When vision, humility, respect, competence, and conviction are at work in the body of Christ, especially across ethnic lines in Christian leadership, there is an ability to tackle real issues in the community. On the other hand, a lack of humility or respect can hinder the work of the Lord not just for one particular church, but for the body of Christ in a city. In my city of Cincinnati, it didn't take me long to realize that there were divides across ethnic lines in the body of Christ from past collaborations that did not reflect humility and respect. This divide has kept leaders from fully trusting each other and working together. There has been a lot of work to rebuild trust from leaders that have been willing to operate with a spirit of vision, humility, respect, competence, and conviction.

Tips for Black Pastors

The need for collaboration is realized when the vision is greater than what one individual church can fulfill. What vision has God put on your heart that is greater than your particular church could accomplish? The idea of bringing the entire body of Christ together in a city may feel a bit daunting. However, you can pray that God brings someone whom you can build a divine connection with. I have seen this in my own city. During the first summer of the COVID-19 pandemic, pastors across our city joined together for protests and prayer. Through these collaborative efforts, I have made some great relationships with White and Asian pastors in our city. We have found ways to encourage and learn from each other and dream about what we could do in the city together. We are just getting started, but perhaps God can do something through these relationships that brings great kingdom impact.

Tips for Leaders Supporting Black Pastors

My challenge for those leaders supporting Black pastors is the same as what I previously mentioned for Black pastors. Identify the vision in your heart that can only be accomplished through collaboration. As you seek to forge these relationships, especially with Black pastors and other pastors of color, make sure that it remains a mutual relationship. Don't just have them meet you on your turf but go to their churches and attend their events. Learn to accept differences as you are making leadership decisions. Live out Romans 12:15 and outdo one another in showing honor.

Tips for Congregants of Black Pastors

It is important that you pray for not only your pastor, but also for the pastors in the city where you live. There are sometimes spiritual forces at work keeping leaders from working together that may not even be identified on the surface. Satan is called the accuser of the brethren! He is constantly bringing accusations against God's people, and it can often derail hopes for collaboration.

I have found that many people in our church love it when they hear of me working with pastors around the city. It brings a sense of safety and encouragement for congregants. If there are opportunities, you may have to lead by example by working with congregants in other churches to make a difference. When you do get these opportunities, find ways to honor what God is doing in their church context no matter the size or ethnic makeup of the church. Keep faith, the pastors will eventually catch up!

Discussion Questions

What are some things that can only be accomplished in this city through collaboration?

What does humility look like between leaders in the body of Christ?

What are some practices that can easily be overlooked that communicate disrespect to people across ethnic lines?

What biases did this chapter reveal?

What fears did this chapter reveal?

Part 3

Hope Alive

10

Modern-Day Examples

I recently read an article by Tom Gjenten called "Multiracial Congregations May Not Bridge the Racial Divide." It discussed the state of multiethnic churches in our nation. The article gives a sobering look at the multiethnic movement that has taken place over the last twenty or so years. It referenced the work of two sociologists, Michael Emerson and Korie Edwards, both of whom have contributed greatly to my research and understanding of this topic.

The article cited some encouraging data, such as the number of multiethnic churches increasing from 6 percent in 1998 to 16 percent in 2019.[59] This number goes even higher within Evangelical churches; in 1998 only 7 percent of their congregations were multiethnic using the 20 percent mark as the measure, and in 2019 there was a significant jump to 23 percent. When they looked at who was leading these churches, there was even more reason for encouragement. In 1998, only 4 percent of multiethnic churches were led by Black pastors, and that number rose to 18 percent in 2019.[60] There is a lot of hope in knowing that people are waking up to the call to be reconciled together in the body of Christ, and this starts with us being able to be in the same place for worship. However, there was another story behind the encouraging numbers.

---

[59] Emerson, Doughtey, et al.
[60] Emerson.

In the midst of the optimism seen in the rise in statistics, Emerson shares some honest critique, admitting that "[all the growth [in multiracial churches] has been people of color moving into white churches. We have seen zero change in the percentage of whites moving into churches of color." Emerson explained further that once a multiracial church becomes less than 50 percent White, the White members leave.[61] He was not the only one quoted in this article with a sobering critique of what has been all too common in multiethnic churches. Korie Edwards remarked, "I came to a point where I realized that, you know, these multiracial churches, just because they're multiracial, doesn't mean they have somehow escaped white supremacy." She continued, saying. "Being diverse doesn't mean that white people are not going to still be in charge and run things."[62] One thing that should be noted about both Emerson and Edwards is that they did not draw their conclusions simply as researchers; both have made steps in their personal lives to be a part of the multiethnic church. When they speak on this subject with these kinds of critiques, they should be taken seriously.

Many of the points that they make can be tied into the questions posed in part 2 of this book. For example, the question of credibility is a significant one to ask if White people are going to go into "churches of color" to follow Black pastors. The question of culture relates to the willingness for the multiethnic churches to be places of integration rather than places of assimilation. The question of conscience deals with whether the multiethnic church will address issues of inequity and concerns of the vulnerable instead of skipping over them in the name of reconciliation.

These are real concerns that need to be addressed, but even with all these concerns, I still have hope for the multiethnic church. I am inspired by the Black pastors I see leading every day. I am inspired by the White pastors who are ready to stand with Black pastors. I am inspired by the opportunity we have as the body of Christ to lead the way in seeking justice and reconciliation in our land. I also recognize that we are just beginning to understand how to live reconciled as the body of Christ in America. If we stay humble and courageous, we can continue to grow into a force of healing in our nation.

---

[61] Gjelten.
[62] Gjelten.

Throughout my journey as a leader of a multiethnic church, I have been grateful for the examples of Black pastors who have mentored me and been sources of inspiration as they've led in multiethnic spaces in the body of Christ. Recently, I was in one of our Mosaix meetings in Cincinnati. This is a group of ministers and leaders in the Cincinnati area committed to catalyzing a movement of leaders who will encourage, resource, and promote the expansion of multiethnic, economically diverse congregations and ministries. In our weekly meeting we discussed some of the challenges that take place when Black pastors desire to see greater diversity in their congregations. As one Black pastor spoke, I could hear the obvious pain and weariness that he had experienced over the years of pursuing a more multiethnic congregation. As he spoke, I was reminded that part of what I experienced in leading our multiethnic church in the same city came on the shoulders of men and women like him who have prayed and labored for churches that are reconciled and diverse. Some of them have not always seen the fruit of their work, like the saints who did not receive what was promised in Hebrews 11, but the labor has not gone in vain.

Many people, in Cincinnati and beyond, have served as mentors, friends, and sources of inspiration for believing in the multiethnic vision. Following is a list of African American pastors who continue to encourage and inspire Chris and me. James Lowe is a pastor who leads a diverse church just outside Nashville, Tennessee. He has spearheaded moments throughout the city to unite people who would have otherwise been at odds with one another. Jon Owens pastors a multiethnic church in the heart of Indianapolis, Indiana, and also creates worship music that reaches beyond cultural divides. Adrian Crawford pastors in Tallahassee, Florida, and has been a force of reconciliation in environments beyond church settings and into the business and sports arenas. Rich Brown is in Abilene, Texas, serving a diverse community, while Donnell Jones pastors and leads in the heart of Washington, DC, pastoring a multiethnic church. Steve Johnson leads a diverse church as an African American pastor in Memphis, Tennessee. Sherman and Melissa Bradley and Chris Woodard pastor multiethnic churches right in Cincinnati, Ohio, and have been allies with me as African American pastors leading multiethnic churches in the same city. Aaron Rooks and his wife are African Americans who have just recently planted a church in Lexington, Kentucky, with a heart to connect people from all throughout the city to be a witness of the kingdom there. There are many others. Among these African American pastors are many varying styles of preaching and leadership, different congregational sizes, and different stages of ministry experience, and yet they lead churches where people from many backgrounds and ethnicities attend.

There are two men in particular who have played a significant role in my development early on as a pastor. One of these men is Brett Fuller. As a student and later as a campus missionary in Every Nation, it mattered to me that I saw someone in leadership that looked like me. Bishop Brett oversees several churches in the Washington, DC, and northern Virginia area that are filled with many different ethnicities and nationalities, including a Korean congregation and a Hispanic congregation. He also serves as the chaplain for the Washington Football team and ministers globally. On top of this, he has helped to govern our global family, Every Nation in many capacities such: National Director for Every Nation here in the United States, member of the Apostolic Council, and board of directors. It seems like there must be more than one of him with the number of things that he does.

Bishop Brett was my first example of what it looked like for a Black man to pastor a church and lead in a ministry with people from all ethnicities. It's not that I did not think it was impossible beforehand; it's that I did not even consider it. In him, I saw a strong Black man with a great family who was unapologetic about being himself. I also saw a man who carried himself with grace and excellence in everything that he did. Several of my peers in ministry have looked to him as a source of encouragement and template of what could be for African American leaders who were ready to lead.

Another leader that I have had the chance to work and minister with on a more personal basis is Tim Johnson. I am grateful for him because in many ways, Pastor Tim became a great spiritual father. He was the man who walked with me on the field for my last football game when my father was unable to make it. He and his wife, Pastor Le'Chelle, counseled my wife and me before we were married, and he officiated the wedding. He was also the pastor we went with to plant a multiethnic church in Orlando, Florida, which may have been one of my most formative experiences as a burgeoning leader.

When I went to Orlando, I witnessed and learned so much about what it looks like to lead a multiethnic church as a Black pastor. I was given the privilege of being up close and personal without having to carry all the weight of the senior pastor. Pastor Tim modeled so many things during these years. As a former NFL athlete, he could relate to the world of the rich and famous, and yet he also had the ability to relate to people in the most broken of circumstances. He is tremendously gifted as a preacher yet had a work ethic like no other. Above all those things, he had a deep love and respect for his wife and family that I have since hoped to model in my own life.

I also saw the challenges of planting a church where all people groups could come. It has been several years since I have been a part of Pastor Tim's church, but it has continued to grow and prosper, and our church in Cincinnati has benefited so much from his influence on my life.

Whether we are looking at examples through history like Lemuel Haynes, Andrew Bryan, or William Seymour, or modern-day examples like Brett Fuller or Tim Johnson, there are great examples of Black leaders pastoring multiethnic churches and ministries. I also see examples beyond the United States, where there are different dynamics in the ethnic divides, but similar calls to bring reconciliation and healing to their respective nations. I think about my friend Pastor Simon Lerefolo, who pastors our Every Nation Church in Johannesburg, South Africa. He has had to lead a multiethnic church through the challenges of racial division in his own nation and has done so with grace and truth. His church has been a beacon of hope not only in South Africa but around the globe.

I am also grateful for the White pastors and pastors of other ethnicities who have encouraged me and other Black pastors in our leadership. There are too many for me to name here, but one of these leaders who has lived the multiethnic vision for decades is Dr. Rice Broocks. He was one of the founders of Every Nation with Dr. Steve Murrell and Pastor Phil Bonasso. With a name like Every Nation, it would not be fitting to be a monoethnic ministry. These men were all White men, but they did not believe in an all-White-led ministry. Many of the Black pastors I mentioned earlier who lead multiethnic churches are part of this movement. Dr. Rice announced in one of his earliest messages at Bethel World Outreach Church, which at the time was a predominantly White congregation, that "[he refused] to pastor an all-White church." He put his money where his mouth was and used his influence and privilege to support African American pastors in their calling. He now calls Pastor James Lowe, an African American, his pastor.

Another source of encouragement is a good friend and mentor, Dr. Steve Murrell. He continues to look for opportunities to open doors for African American pastors and pastors of all ethnicities to lead within our very diverse worldwide movement. He has spoken up when tough issues related to race have surfaced in our nation and in the world, even at the risk of being misunderstood himself. I am grateful for his courageous efforts to develop leaders from all ethnic backgrounds and create spaces for them to lead.

I also think about my good friends Lance Phillips and Brock Lillis, who both lead great multicultural churches in Clarksville and Murfreesboro, Tennessee, respectively. Both these men have empowered leaders from other ethnicities to truly lead major aspects of their ministry and share the pulpit. We have spent countless hours on phone calls talking through painful realities and praying for healing in our land. My friend Brock grew up much differently than me in a town called Philadelphia, Mississippi. His family came from an environment where racism and bigotry were normal, but when Jesus changed his heart, he became an ambassador of reconciliation. Many years ago, we both stood in front of our ministry peers for a moment of identificational repentance, and we watched God heal something in the hearts of those who were there. I am thankful for the men of God that I walk with, and I am hopeful for the reconciliation coming out of their churches.

When I was getting ready to plant our church in Cincinnati, I met Chris Beard, a pastor of a well-respected and diverse church there. He experienced firsthand the opportunities and challenges of leading a predominately White congregation to one of the most diverse churches in our area. It meant a lot for me to hear him as a White pastor speak on the importance Black pastors planting churches in the city where he had ministered for so long: "We need Black pastors leading multiethnic churches to break the back of the enemy over racism in the church."

Let me close out this chapter by honoring the team that has built with me in Cincinnati. We are not a large team, but we are a very diverse team with a large vision. Every pastor probably feels like she or he has the best staff ever, but our staff must at least be close. We have wrestled together through difficult discussions. We have risked offending each other for the sake of deeper unity. There has been an openness to grow, especially concerning issues that are racially charged. Some of my White team members have been misunderstood by other White people for speaking out on issues that concern communities that do not directly affect them. Other staff members who do not identify as either Black or White have patiently pressed in to understand the depth of the wounds of our racial history in the United States. When I walk into our church service and see it filled with people from different backgrounds, I know it is not window dressing. We don't just meet together, we eat together.

11

A Fresh Commitment and Warning

Over the years, I have come to appreciate the diversity in our church more and more. There is nothing cheap about what it costs to consistently build with believers who look different, vote different, and see the world differently than you do. Diversity is a good idea until it costs you something. It cost Jesus His blood (Revelation 5:9), and it costs us our privilege and comfort. I have seen the beauty and power that comes when people who don't know the Lord come into a service and witness a community of people worshiping together and loving one another. I am also aware of the dangers that can come for anyone leading or anyone who is part of a team leading a multiethnic church. The word danger may seem a bit dramatic since the dream of a church that reaches diverse groups of people is a God idea, not a man's idea. Planting a church in creative access areas where Christianity is persecuted can be dangerous, serving people who are deeply broken can be dangerous, but is building a multiethnic church "dangerous"?

Well, there are some things we need to be warned about, so I've made a list of dangers that face leaders of multiethnic churches, and it is as much for me as it is for anyone reading this right now.

1. **The danger of overestimating our progress.** In many ways, being part of a multiethnic church is a sign of progress. For those

who have pastored in such a context, it is clear that God's hand must build it. However, there are real racial biases and systemic issues in our culture that still exist. We would be unwise to believe that those mindsets and systems are void in our churches just because the church has different ethnic groups in attendance. Don't think that people in your church are insulated from those same challenges. You can go to a diverse church and still be bigoted or have biased attitudes. I often find that social media keeps me sobered about our true progress. Let's celebrate our progress while being honest about the work that still needs to be done in our community and in our church.

2. **The danger of seeing multiethnic churches as the end and not the means.** When our churches have diversity, that is a big win, but it is not the end game. Multiethnic churches have a tremendous opportunity to be forces of healing and reconciliation in our communities. Along with that, and perhaps even more important, we have an opportunity to fulfill the great commission to make disciples of all nations by being a community that both welcomes and disciples diverse populations. At the end of the day, our multiethnic churches should result in kingdom advancement beyond the walls of the church.

3. **The danger of playing it safe for the sake of unity.** I know the angst that comes when a racially charged event takes place on a Saturday night. I know that something needs to be said. I know that someone is going to be mad. The safest thing is to avoid the topic or speak so generally that I really say nothing. What if I say a comment that drives away all the people of a particular group? We should listen to others and continually grow so that we can speak with wisdom and grace. There are times when it is better to wait for greater clarity from God before speaking and acting. However, let's not confuse our lack of courage with wisdom. We must be willing to speak up and step up when the moment calls for it.

4. **The danger of settling for assimilation rather than integration.** Here's a question to consider: who has to adjust most and who has to adjust least when becoming part of your church? Many churches can unknowingly have one dominant culture that minorities to

have to assimilate into while leaving no room for these same groups to help shape the culture of the church. In the book *United by Faith*, Karen Kim, Curtiss DeYoung, Michael Emerson, and George Yancey do a masterful job of distinguishing between assimilated multiethnic churches, pluralistic churches, and integrated churches. I have heard many people say, "Everyone is welcome at our church." What they sometimes mean is, "Everyone who is willing to assimilate into our culture is welcome at our church."

5. **The danger of being color-blind.** If we celebrate one group, does that mean we do not love other groups? We taught our kids early on that it's OK to celebrate one kid without celebrating all the kids at that moment. This is a sign of maturity as kids grow, and it is a sign of maturity as churches grow, too. Instead of downplaying or ignoring our differences, what if we learned to celebrate our unique histories and rich cultures in a way that brings value, not division?

6. **The danger of ignoring specific needs of minority groups.** One of the blessings that has resulted from homogeneous churches is that the needs of many minority communities are met in ways that mainstream culture is unable to do. It was in the Black church that I learned Black history and gained a healthy sense of how people who look like me have contributed to this great nation. We must learn in our multiethnic churches to grab hold of one thing (multiethnic ministry) without letting go of the other (understanding the unique needs of differing groups). This goes back to our willingness to celebrate each other, and I admit that this is not always easy.

7. **The danger of self-righteousness.** If there is one thing that bothers God more than a lack of diversity, it is a lack of humility. Proverbs 18:12 reminds us: "Before destruction the heart of man is haughty, but humility goes before honor." As leaders of multiethnic churches, we are not better than pastors of homogeneous churches. I believe in building the way we do as a church, but we cannot subtly take on superiority complexes. Our call is to be faithful with the opportunities that God has given us.

12

I Still Have Hope

In a recent sermon that spoke to the ethnic tension in our land during the writing of this book, my co-author Chris Johnson said, "We were built for this." Where can the world look to for an example of true reconciliation? Our society understands a form of tolerance that says, "you do you, and I will do me." There is a tolerance that says we can be in the same space and live within our own silos without significant interactions with people who look or think outside your circle. Yet this form of tolerance is a cheapened version of what the kingdom of God offers.

The book of Revelation gives the church the opportunity to build with the end in mind. In Revelation 7:9, we get a behind the scenes look at heaven: "After these things I looked, and behold, a great multitude which no one could count, from every nation and all tribes and peoples and tongues, standing before the throne and before the Lamb." This eschatological picture from John shows us people from all types of ethnicities and backgrounds connected with one purpose: worshiping Jesus the lamb. Since Jesus told us to pray, "Thy Kingdom come on earth as it is in heaven," one of the ways the church can seek to be a reflection of this heavenly picture is to build multiethnic worship communities.

Several years ago, I had the opportunity to go to Kingston, Jamaica, three times in the same year for ministry work. I fell in love with the culture, the people, and the food. Now that I live in Cincinnati, trips to Kingston are not as frequent for me. However, I do have a favorite Jamaican spot right in Uptown Cincinnati that I have gone to many times. When you go there, you hear the island music, the colors of Jamaica are plastered over the walls, and you can order oxtail, jerk chicken, and beef patties. If I want people in Cincinnati to get a taste of Jamaica, I can either buy them a passport and a ticket, or I can buy them a meal. As believers, we should be a taste of heaven on earth. Ryan Storey, the South African preacher and author of the book *With God in the Crucible,* challenged the church with these words: "The richest gift the Church can give the world is to be different from it."[63]

If we are going to take the Matthew 28:19 mandate to disciple the nations seriously, then we must find ways to empower leaders from different nations and ethnicities. Our churches, and paraministries as well, need people from all ethnicities who are able to lead them. It is only then that we can truly benefit from the whole body of Christ. Latino pastors have something to say to Latinos and non-Latinos alike. White pastors have something to say to White people and non-Whites alike. Our Asian pastors need to speak to Asians and non-Asians alike. And Black pastors have something of value to say to Black people and non-Black people alike. As we continue to pursue the vision of a multiethnic church and champion the voices of Black pastors and leaders, my prayer is that the church in America would grow to wholeheartedly embrace unity while celebrating ethnic diversity. May we come together to bridge racial divides and be reconciled with each other, and may the church illustrate that love is stronger than hatred. I still have hope.

The burden to lead or plant multiethnic churches must come from a prophetic picture of the Word of God active in the world. Making the effort to lead multiethnic churches, we are making a statement saying that we are willing to walk in the prophetic pictures of the bride of Christ. The church is a spiritual organism with practical purposes to help people experience God, be transformed by God, and reconciled to one another. This book is meant to encourage anyone who wants to support the equality of the gospel in a divided world that thrives on inequality. When this happens, principalities, ideologies, systems, and structures are called into the accountability of Christ.

---

[63] Storey, Chapter 2, *With God in the Crucible*

Afterword

Why Parts of This Book May Offend You

As much as I am excited for this book to be in the hands of people and a resource to bless the body of Christ, admittedly I had a bit of reticence while writing this book. For those who do not know me or Chris personally, there could be some assumptions about our intentions and our viewpoints because as we mention, this topic is rarely engaged without emotion. There is also a realization that somewhere down the line we may be off without even realizing it. Perhaps there were points where our tone was not what it should have been, or we failed to say as much as needed to be said. I pray that the Holy Spirit will be the supernatural translator to the readers of this book and give you the ability to take the parts that are helpful and spit out the bones on the parts that are not. I also pray that God gives each and every reader the ability to hear His voice even at the points of this book that may seem hard to accept.

I also know that books like these have an ability to age in different ways. Over the years some of these questions that we addressed may change, shift in significance, or altogether disappear. New questions may arise. Quite frankly, my hope is that decades from now we are not still wrestling with the same challenges in the body of Christ as it relates to multiethnic churches. This book is but one resource out of many to help us better reflect the kingdom of God on earth as it is in heaven.

Perhaps you feel as though too much emphasis is placed on issues of race in the body of Christ. If we just stick to the gospel, then everything else will work its way out. In one sense I agree with this sentiment. If we can stick with the gospel, then God will change situations from the inside out. The problem comes when we are blinded to our cultural, historical, and personal biases that keep us from seeing the gospel in its fullest sense. It is possible to genuinely love Jesus and simultaneously perpetuate barriers that work against people walking in the call that God has for their lives.

Finally, I understand that there is still much more to say on this topic. I believe that the principles in this book have application to a variety of contexts, but they are still limited in focus. How does this apply to those in the caste system in different parts of India? What impact does this book have on those who live and minister in a postapartheid South Africa? How about empowering leaders amidst the tribal tensions in Kenya? By the way, are these the same questions women leading multiethnic churches face as well? Perhaps this is a hint toward the next book that is coming, or the next book that you are supposed to write. Our hope is that *Ready to Lead* encourages the body of Christ in this journey of learning and growing.

Notes

1. Emerson, Michael O., and Christian Smith. *Divided by Faith : Evangelical Religion and the Problem of Race in America*. Oxford: Oxford University Press, 2000.
2. Emerson 2020
3. Excerpt from Mosaix Global Network, newsletter, December 2019
4. Gjelten, NPR "Multiracial Congregations May Not Bridge Racial Divide"
5. James Baldwin, "I Am Not Your Negro"
6. Hatch, Nathan O. *The Democratization of American Christianity*. Reprint edition, Yale University Press, 1991, pg 106. Raboteau, Albert J. *Slave Religion: The "Invisible Institution" in the Antebellum South*. Updated edition, Oxford University Press, 2004, pg 133.
7. Anyabwile, Thabiti M., and John Piper. *The Faithful Preacher (Foreword by John Piper): Recapturing the Vision of Three Pioneering African-American Pastors*. Crossway, 2007, pg 18.
8. Anyabwile, Thabiti M., and John Piper. *The Faithful Preacher (Foreword by John Piper): Recapturing the Vision of Three Pioneering African-American Pastors*. Crossway, 2007, pg 20.
9. Raboteau, Albert J. *Slave Religion: The "Invisible Institution" in the Antebellum South*. Updated edition, Oxford University Press, 2004, pg 134.
10. Woodson, Carter G. *The History of the Negro Church*. The Associated Publishers, 1921, pg 55.
11. Woodson, Carter G. *The History of the Negro Church*. The Associated Publishers, 1921, pg 47-48.
12. Woodson, Carter G. *The History of the Negro Church*. The Associated Publishers, 1921, pg 49-52.

13. Woodson, Carter G. *The History of the Negro Church*. The Associated Publishers, 1921, pg 55-56.
14. Woodson, Carter G. *The History of the Negro Church*. The Associated Publishers, 1921, pg 56.
15. Raboteau, Albert J. *Slave Religion: The "Invisible Institution" in the Antebellum South*. Updated edition, Oxford University Press, 2004, pg 134.
16. Raboteau, Albert J. *Slave Religion: The "Invisible Institution" in the Antebellum South*. Updated edition, Oxford University Press, 2004, pg 135.
17. Hatch, Nathan O. *The Democratization of American Christianity*. Reprint edition, Yale University Press, 1991, pg 106. Raboteau, Albert J. *Slave Religion: The "Invisible Institution" in the Antebellum South*. Updated edition, Oxford University Press, 2004, pg 106.
18. Woodson, Carter G. *The History of the Negro Church*. The Associated Publishers, 1921, pg 69.
19. Woodson, Carter G. *The History of the Negro Church*. The Associated Publishers, 1921, pg 63.
20. Hatch, Nathan O. *The Democratization of American Christianity*. Reprint edition, Yale University Press, 1991, pg 106. Raboteau, Albert J. *Slave Religion: The "Invisible Institution" in the Antebellum South*. Updated edition, Oxford University Press, 2004, pg 49.
21. Hatch, Nathan O. *The Democratization of American Christianity*. Reprint edition, Yale University Press, 1991, pg 106. Raboteau, Albert J. *Slave Religion: The "Invisible Institution" in the Antebellum South*. Updated edition, Oxford University Press, 2004, pg 50.
22. "More on Leaving White Evangelicalism: A Response from Bryan Loritts." *The Exchange | A Blog by Ed Stetzer*,
23. Middleton, Lorenzo. "Black Professors on White Campuses." *Chronicle of Higher Education*, vol. 63, no. 11, Nov. 2016, pp 30.
24. Middleton, Lorenzo. "Black Professors on White Campuses." *Chronicle of Higher Education*, vol. 63, no. 11, Nov. 2016, pp 30.
25. Basow, Susan A., et al. "The Effects of Professors' Race and Gender on Student Evaluations and Performance." *College Student Journal*, vol. 47, no. 2, Summer 2013, pp. 352. *EBSCOhost*.

26. Basow, Susan A., et al. "The Effects of Professors' Race and Gender on Student Evaluations and Performance." *College Student Journal*, vol. 47, no. 2, Summer 2013, pp. 354.
27. Keller, Tim, et al. *Race And the Christian: An Evening with John Piper and Tim Keller, Moderated by Anthony Bradley.*
28. Loritts, Bryan. *Insider Outsider: My Journey as a Stranger in White Evangelicalism and My Hope for Us All.* Zondervan, 2018.
29. DeYoung, Curtiss Paul, et al. *United by Faith: The Multiracial Congregation As an Answer to the Problem of Race.* 1 edition, Oxford University Press, 2004, pp 165.
30. DeYoung, Curtiss Paul, et al. *United by Faith: The Multiracial Congregation As an Answer to the Problem of Race.* 1 edition, Oxford University Press, 2004, pp 165.
31. DeYoung, Curtiss Paul, et al. *United by Faith: The Multiracial Congregation As an Answer to the Problem of Race.* 1 edition, Oxford University Press, 2004, pp 165-166.
32. Gushiken, Kevin M. "Paulo Freire and His Contribution to Multiethnic Churches." *To Cite This Article: Kevin M. Gushiken (2012) Paulo Freire and His Contribution to Multiethnic Churches, Religious Education, 107:2, 122-138, DOI: 10.1080/00344087.2012.660415 To Link to This Article: Http://Dx.Doi.Org/10.1080/00344087.2012.6604*, 2012, pp. 122–38, http://dx.doi.org/10.1080/00344087.2012.660415.
33. Barron, Jessica M. "Managed Diversity: Race, Place, and an Urban Church." *Sociology of Religion*, vol. 77, no. 1, Spring 2016, pp. 26. *EBSCOhost*, doi:10.1093/socrel/srv074.
34. Barron, Jessica M. "Managed Diversity: Race, Place, and an Urban Church." *Sociology of Religion*, vol. 77, no. 1, Spring 2016, pp.27. *EBSCOhost*, doi:10.1093/socrel/srv074.
35. Alcántara, Jared E. *Crossover Preaching: Intercultural-Improvisational Homiletics in Conversation with Gardner C. Taylor.* IVP Academic, 2015, pp 160.
36. Howell, Brian M., and Jenell Williams Paris. "The Concept of Culture." *Introducing Cultural Anthroplogy: A Chrstian Perspective*, Baker Academic, 2011, pp. 27.

37. Usry, Glenn, and Craig S. Keener. *Black Man's Religion: Can Christianity Be Afrocentric?* PRINT-ON-DEMAND edition, IVP Academic, 1996, pp. 17.
38. Edwards, Korie L., and Rebecca Kim. "Estranged Pioneers: The Case of African American and Asian American Multiracial Church Pastors." *Sociology of Religion: A Quarterly Review 2019*, Jan. 2019, pp. 215, https://doi.org/10.1093/socrel/sry059.
39. Edwards, Korie L. The Elusive Dream: The Power of Race in Interacial Churches. Oxford University Press, 2008, pp 66.
40. Edwards, Korie L. Christerson, Brad, and Emerson, Michael. "Race, Religious Organizations, and Integration." Annual Review of Sociology, vol. 39, 2013, pp 221.
41. Alexander, Claude and Leith Anderson. "What White Christians Need to Know about Black Churches." *NAE.Org*, 15 Jan. 2017, http://zotero.org/support/quick_start_guide.
42. Carter, Niambi, and Pearl Dowe. "The Racial Exceptionalism of Barack Obama." *Journal of African American Studies*, vol. 19, no. 2, June 2015, pp. 106. *EBSCOhost*, doi:10.1007/s12111-015-9298-9.
43. Carter, Niambi, and Pearl Dowe. "The Racial Exceptionalism of Barack Obama." *Journal of African American Studies*, vol. 19, no. 2, June 2015, pp. 106. *EBSCOhost*, doi:10.1007/s12111-015-9298-9.
44. Carter, Niambi, and Pearl Dowe. "The Racial Exceptionalism of Barack Obama." *Journal of African American Studies*, vol. 19, no. 2, June 2015, pp. 106. *EBSCOhost*, doi:10.1007/s12111-015-9298-9.
45. Carter, Niambi, and Pearl Dowe. "The Racial Exceptionalism of Barack Obama." *Journal of African American Studies*, vol. 19, no. 2, June 2015, pp. 109. *EBSCOhost*, doi:10.1007/s12111-015-9298-9. Terry, Brandon. "Racial Politics After Obama." *Dissent (00123846)*, vol. 63, no. 3, Summer 2016, pp. 48-49. *EBSCOhost*, http://ezproxy.asburyseminary.edu/login?url=http://search.ebscohost.com/login.aspx?direct=true&db=slh&AN=116824875&site=eds-live.
46. Coates, Ta-Nehisi. "My President Was Black. (Cover Story)." *Atlantic*, vol. 319, no. 1, Feb. 2017, p. 56, 66. *EBSCOhost*, http://ezproxy.asburyseminary.edu/login?url=http://search.ebscohost.com/login.aspx?direct=true&db=ulh&AN=119832561&site=eds-live.

47. Carter, Niambi, and Pearl Dowe. "The Racial Exceptionalism of Barack Obama." *Journal of African American Studies*, vol. 19, no. 2, June 2015, pp. 108. *EBSCOhost*, doi:10.1007/s12111-015-9298-9.
48. Coates, Ta-Nehisi. "My President Was Black. (Cover Story)." *Atlantic*, vol. 319, no. 1, Feb. 2017, p. 63. *EBSCOhost*, http://ezproxy.asburyseminary.edu/login?url=http://search.ebscohost.com/login.aspx?direct=true&db=ulh&AN=119832561&site=eds-live.
49. Carter, Niambi, and Pearl Dowe. "The Racial Exceptionalism of Barack Obama." *Journal of African American Studies*, vol. 19, no. 2, June 2015, pp. 109. *EBSCOhost*, doi:10.1007/s12111-015-9298-9. Terry, Brandon. "Racial Politics After Obama." *Dissent (00123846)*, vol. 63, no. 3, Summer 2016, pp. 48-49. *EBSCOhost*, http://ezproxy.asburyseminary.edu/login?url=http://search.ebscohost.com/login.aspx?direct=true&db=slh&AN=116824875&site=eds-live.
50. Terry, Brandon. "Racial Politics After Obama." *Dissent (00123846)*, vol. 63, no. 3, Summer 2016, pp. 49. *EBSCOhost*, http://ezproxy.asburyseminary.edu/login?url=http://search.ebscohost.com/login.aspx?direct=true&db=slh&AN=116824875&site=eds-live.
51. Cooper, Brittney. "Stop Poisoning the Race Debate: How 'Respectability Politics' Rears Its Ugly Head — Again." *Salon*, 18 Mar. 2015, https://www.salon.com/2015/03/18/stop_poisoning_the_race_debate_how_respectability_politics_rears_its_ugly_head_again/.
52. Dyson, Michael Eric. *The Black Presidency: Barack Obama and the Politics of Race in America*. 1 edition, Houghton Mifflin Harcourt, 2016, pp 5.
53. Storey, Peter. With God in the Crucible: Preaching Costly Discipleship. Abingdon Press. 2002.
54. Ward, David. Practicing the Preaching Life. Abingdon Press, 2019, pp 76.
55. Taylor, Gardner. Lecture to Harvard Divinity School on Preaching: Youtube location: https://www.youtube.com/watch?v=WPBgvg2CI8k&t=451s
56. Okesson, Gregg. *DM 911 Doctoral Class at Asbury Theological Seminary: Discovering God's Missional Heart*. Doctor of Ministry Class: Discovering God's Missional Heart (August 10, 2017).
57. Chan, Francis, *Until Unity*, David Cook, 2021, pp 96
58. Index, Youth and Families, February 2016

59. Dougherty, Kevin and Emerson, Michael. The Changing Complexion of American Congregations. Journal for the Scientific Study of Religion, 2016.
60. Emerson, Michael O., and Christian Smith. *Divided by Faith : Evangelical Religion and the Problem of Race in America*. Oxford: Oxford University Press, 2000.
61. Gjelten, NPR "Multiracial Congregations May Not Bridge Racial Divide"
62. Gjelten, NPR "Multiracial Congregations May Not Bridge Racial Divide"
63. Storey, Peter. With God in the Crucible: Preaching Costly Discipleship. Abingdon Press. 2002.